HOW TO READ THE BIBLE

How
to
Read
the
Bible

JAMES A. FISCHER

This edition first published by Prentice-Hall, Inc.,
Englewood Cliffs, New Jersey 07632, USA, 1987

UK edition published 1988

British Library Cataloguing in Publication Data

Fischer, James
    How to read the Bible. — Rev. ed.
    1. Bible — Critical studies
    I. Title
    220.6

    ISBN 1-85274-038-8

*Crucible is an imprint of the Aquarian Press, part of the
Thorsons Publishing Group, Wellingborough, Northamptonshire,
NN8 2RQ, England.*

Printed in Great Britain by Biddles Limited, Guildford, Surrey

10   9   8   7   6   5   4   3   2   1

JAMES A. FISCHER, a former president of the Catholic Biblical Association of America, is Professor of New Testament at St. Thomas Seminary, Denver. He has written numerous articles on the Bible, religion in life today, and related topics, and is the author of several books.

Contents

ONE

Getting Acquainted with the Bible

GETTING REACQUAINTED WITH THE BIBLE

You are probably reading this book because you already know the Bible. It is valuable, therefore, to assess your previous experience before considering a new one. Many of us first encountered the Bible in church services. That may have put the Bible into a very formidable place where we keep sacred things. We may have heard the Bible as part of our childhood discipline and think of it as a catalog of dos and don'ts that are not to be questioned. That also makes it rather formidable. On the other hand, the Bible may have been quite remote from us in our religious upbringing, a book to be respected but not read. Our initial attempts to read it may have been unsatisfactory for many reasons; we may have found it not to make much sense, or we may have found it making statements with which we disagreed. These are broad observations, perhaps even caricatures in your experience. They do raise some questions, however, and it might be well to stop right here and allow yourself time to reflect on just how you have viewed the Bible in your previous experience.

Part of our problem is to separate our reverential feelings from our ordinary attitudes toward reading. Perhaps one way to do this would be to read someone else's sacred books. Certainly we would want to be reverential because others hold these books as sacred and try to live by them. Nonetheless, we could more easily read their books as literature and be aware of how the various styles of writing affect us. The Book of Mormon, for example, is an account of what is said to have happened between 600 B.C. and 421 A.D. to a group of migrating Jews. After a brief introduction of the author, Nephi, the Book of Mormon begins with a story: "For it came to pass in the commencement of the first year of the reign of Zedekiah, king of Judah (my father, Lehi, having dwelt at Jerusalem in all his days); and in that same year there came many prophets, prophesying unto the people that they must repent, or the great city Jerusalem must be destroyed." The story thus begun continues to unfold through the whole book. Along the way the Book of Mormon evolves a strong moral point: the stories fall into cycles of virtue that lead to prosperity, then to pride and inequity among people, and so on to God's chastisement and the people's repentance. The beliefs of this people are carried along by a story.

The Rig Veda of Hinduism, on the other hand, is a collection of hymns to various gods. "We meditate on the lovely light of the god, Savitri. May it stimulate our thoughts." Praise and meditation are the obvious purpose of this book. It is not the only sacred book in the Hindu religion; there are many more, such as the Upanishads, which tend to be philosophical inquiries. Story plays but a small part except for an occasional bit of myth. For example, the second chapter of the Bridhadāranyaka Upanishad begins: "In the beginning nothing at all existed here. This [the whole world] was enveloped by Death, by Hunger. For what is Death but Hunger? And [Death] bethought himself: 'Would that I had a self.' He roamed around, offering praise; and from him, as he offered praise, water was born. And he said [to himself]: 'Yes, it was a joy to me to offer praise.' And this is what makes fire fire. And joy is the lot of him who understands that this is what makes fire fire." Whatever this style of writing may do for us, it certainly sends a strong signal that we are in unfamiliar territory, a world in which measurement and action and logic are not paramount.

If we can stand back far enough from the Bible to read it as literature, we discover a veritable kaleidoscope of forms and styles. As one opens the Bible, stories pour out from it. There are the stories of creation, of the flood, of the tower of Babel, of Abraham and Joseph, and of the exodus from Egypt. Many of them are quite clear; others seem fragmentary and poorly connected within the stream of narrative. Into this matrix of story come law and custom that describe the lifestyle of a people. As the story continues over the centuries, prophets begin to challenge the people to return to their original declaration of ideals. Sermons come into the literature; most of these prophetic writings are also fragmentary. Conclusions and basic themes are given, but the rest is left to the reader to fill in. Later (or perhaps meanwhile) writers of reflective mind are catching up the sayings of the common people and probing deeper into that wisdom. Such are the main kinds of writing that one finds in the Old Testament, though this short cataloging does not do justice to its richness. The New Testament more or less reproduces the same types. Stories abound in the Gospels, wise reflections in the Epistles and always there is a prophetic call to a lifestyle which constantly eludes full accomplishment.

Whatever may be said of all of this writing, it is evidently a record of what various people experienced. It has a lifelike quality. Like life itself, it is never complete; more remains to be learned. Each writing is a benchmark for the surveyor of life, a blaze cut in a tree for the explorer, a flag planted on a rise in the land for the warrior. It is immensely human, deeply "gut-level," always challenging. The Bible has had that effect even at secondhand. The image of the Good Samaritan survives in our culture even outside the Bible and challenges us to go and do in like manner. Even the restful images challenge. "The Lord is my shepherd; I shall not want." (Psalm 23:1) The security promised challenges whether we can accept it. The Bible is not a safe book if you are looking solely for consolation or immediate justification. As literature it is too authentically human to allow an escape without a response.

Such is the book with which you must become comfortable before reading too far. It is a deeply disturbing book which nonetheless asks us to join the human race. It asks us to confront ourselves. It even asks us to confront the God who is presented in its pages. Such is the

gist of the dialogue of Job and the musings of Koheleth. Such also is
the story of the woman who kept pestering the unjust judge until he
heard her case; (Luke 18:1–8); in this wise we must take our stance
if we pray to the God of the Bible. If you are going to read the Bible
at all, whether you believe in it or not, you must be prepared to come
to grips with a whole host of combatants, including God himself. Yet
this is what makes victory possible and yields the ultimate consolation
of seizing upon reality and advancing in the quest of mystery. The
book is a book of life—the life of the people who wrote it, and
eventually of the people who read it.

   The Bible is different from other books. It is different from other
sacred books in its content and general style of procedure. It is different
from secular books. It takes itself seriously and it takes you seriously.
It may well be different from your previous impressions about the
Bible. That remains to be discovered as you read this book about the
Bible.

GETTING FAMILIAR WITH THE TEXT

   Many people have a favorite Bible. It may be a favorite because
it is a family heirloom. It is apt to be the King James Version in a
Protestant family or a Douay-Rheims Version in a Roman Catholic
family. It is not apt to be very easy to read since these translations are
three or four hundred years old. They have familiar phrases which we
are reluctant to give up; our whole English culture has been affected
by them and they are sometimes part of our usual speech. However,
over the long run reading the old translations creates additional difficulties since much of their style and wording is remote from our way
of writing and conversing. For the purposes of this book it would be
better to read a modern translation. The study of ancient languages
and textual criticism have made great progress in the past century;
new archaeological discoveries have enabled us to understand the ancient texts far better. In addition, one disturbing bone of contention
among different sects of Christians has been downplayed; in the scholarly community the distinctions between "Protestant" and "Catholic"

Bibles have been all but wiped out and this is filtering down to the popular level. Some of the new translations appear in ecumenical editions; all of them are honest efforts to translate accurately what the original text said. In an unexpected way we are closer to having one Bible these days, although it appears in a multiplicity of translations. It is helpful to know something of the virtues and limitations of these Bibles, either to select one for the purpose one has in mind or to become aware of the intentions of the translators of one's favorite Bible.

The New English Bible (NEB)

The New English Bible began to appear in 1961, the work of a group of British scholars who had the backing of almost all the Protestant and Reformed Churches in Great Britain. It is now available in an ecumenical edition (1970). NEB was not planned as another revision of the revered King James Version, but as a new beginning which aimed at accuracy with flexibility. The Introduction to the New Testament states: "Taken as a whole, our version claims to be a translation, free, it may be, rather than literal, but a faithful translation nevertheless as far as we could compass it." The English style is contemporary British, although the traditional "thee" and "thou" for God has been retained. The men who made it knew the possibilities of our very rich English idiom. This is a Bible to be enjoyed for the felicity and fluidity of its English readings. Since it is British, it sometimes has that peculiar flavor for American readers. By and large, however, it is both a delightful English text and a faithful rendering of the original languages.

The problems with NEB are mostly technical. Any translator must make innumerable decisions as to what text shall be translated. For centuries there has been only one standard Hebrew text of the Old Testament, called the Massoretic Text. However, in recent years archaeological discoveries at Qumran, Ras Shamra, in Phoenicia, Mesopotamia and Egypt have yielded linguistic data that enables us to check and sometimes improve on the Massoretic Text. The situation with the New Testament has always been more complex because there has been not one textual tradition but at least three major families of texts and hundreds of individual manuscripts with tens of thousands of variants. It is still the most accurate text handed down from antiquity, but it does offer the translator numerous choices from which to translate. The temptation of NEB has been to be rather adventurous in this field, both in the Old Testament and the New. Although the translation is satisfactorily literal, the text from which the translator worked was often conjectural. One should not be surprised, then, if NEB reads differently at times from other Bibles. It is not just a choice of English words that makes the difference.

New American Bible (NAB)

This translation was published in 1970, the work of American Roman Catholic scholars under the supervision of the Catholic Biblical Association. The aim is stated in the Preface: "From the original and oldest available texts of the sacred books, (this translation) aims to convey as directly as possible the thought and individual style of the inspired writers." The style is clear, straightforward, unpretentious, and unexciting American English. The translation is not slavish; indeed, at times, it is more interpretative than literal. The translators aimed at conveying "the individual style of the inspired authors," but it may be questioned how well they succeeded. The translation of Paul sounds more like the individual translators than like Paul. However, the emphasis was on reliability rather than on readability. In that area NAB rates high marks. The variants which are followed in the Old Testament and the New are usually judiciously chosen from the latest research data. The footnotes, it may be added, reflect Roman Catholic interests; the text is without sectarian slant. In this book the NAB will be used unless otherwise noted. A new edition of NAB for reading in church with improved attention to public reading is in the process of publication.

The Jerusalem Bible (JB)

Alexander Jones translated the French version called *La Bible de Jerusalem*, a product of the Dominican Fathers of the *Ecole Biblique* in

Jerusalem. The English translation first appeared in 1966 and since then there have been translations into many other languages. The popularity of the English version seems to depend on two quite extraneous factors: Alexander Jones was able to mold a fluent and intelligent form on the English translation, and second, the introductory explanations and the footnotes from the original French are of extremely high quality. The translation is fairly accurate although it shows a preference in the Old Testament for readings based on the ancient versions in Greek, Coptic, and so on. For the general reader it is a good and pleasant translation; if it pleases, it should be used.

The Good News Bible (GNB)*

The complete Good News Bible appeared in 1976, the work of a group of American biblical scholars under the sponsorship of the American Bible Society. The aim of the translators is stated in the Foreword: "The Bible in Today's English Version is a new translation which seeks to state clearly and accurately the meaning of the original texts in words and forms that are widely accepted by people who use English as a means of communication. This translation does not follow the traditional vocabulary and style found in the historic English Bible versions. Rather it attempts in this century to set forth the Biblical content and message in a standard, everyday, natural form of English." The GNB succeeds to a remarkable degree in doing so. However, as in all translations which are a group project, the success varies from book to book. Some of the Old Testament has been criticized for not using the most modern textual analysis available. For the New Testament a new critical edition of the Greek was first prepared and this has been of great help. Even so, the English interpretation can sometimes leave one questioning whether that was what the Greek intended to say. All in all, GNB is a valuable translation, accurate and forthright.

*Also called Today's English Version; the New Testament is also published under the title Good News for Modern Man.

If you like your Bible to be idiomatic, though not racy, this may be the one for you.

The Living Bible (LB)

Kenneth Taylor has produced a different kind of version which he calls a "paraphrase-translation." Instead of beginning with a committee of scholars who slowly mine their way out of the pit of ancient texts to a modern translation and then hand it over to literary editors to write out the inevitable "committeese," Taylor reversed the process. He alone paraphrased the American Standard Version to give what he considered the meaning of whole sentences and passages. Then he handed it over to the biblical scholars to check for accuracy. The result has been an immensely popular book. Whether accuracy can be assured by such doubling back is very questionable. The tendency is to read in opinions which are present before the text is designed. Taylor admits this. "When the Greek or Hebrew is not clear, then the theology of the translator is his guide, along with his sense of logic, unless perchance the translation is allowed to stand without any clear meaning at all. The theological lodestar in this book has been a rigid evangelical position." Scholars shy away from the book for its numerous questionable readings.

King James Version (KJV)

The King James Version was first published in 1611, the work of the best scholars at Westminister, Oxford, and Cambridge. The translation, which relied on much work that had been done earlier by Anglicans, Lutherans, Calvinists, and Catholics, was favorably received and was authorized to be read (hence the usual subtitle: Authorized Version). The original dedication to King James of Great Britain, France, and Ireland stated: "For when Your Highness had once out of deep judgment apprehended how convenient it was that out of the Original Sacred Tongues, together with comparing of the labours, both in our own, and other foreign Languages, of many worthy men who went before us, there should be one more exact Translation of the holy

Scriptures into the English Tongue; Your Majesty did never desist to urge and to excite those to whom it was commended, that the work might be hastened, and that the business might be expedited in so decent a manner, as a matter of such importance might justly require." By seventeenth-century standards the translation was commendably faithful to the original texts then available. Oddly enough, the English phrasing was first resisted as barbarous, but in the course of time, came to assert itself as the very model of English diction. As the dedication noted above indicates, political and sectarian purposes had considerable influence on the translators. The original footnotes, which were intensely polemical, have now been dropped. The reader's judgment about using the King James Version will probably depend on how high a priority is given to previous familiarity with the text as a cherished tradition.

New Jewish Version (NJV)

The New Jewish Version is being produced by a group of scholars under the auspices of the Jewish Publication Society. *The Torah, The Five Books of Moses* was published in 1962, *The Five Scrolls* in 1969, *The Psalms* in 1972, and *The Prophets* in 1978, and *The Writings* in 1982. An earlier Jewish translation of the Old Testament had been in reality a slight revision of the English Revised Version of the King James. NJV aimed at departing from this traditional English language, but an inner longing of the translators sometimes inhibited them. Thus "Thee-Thou" were dropped, but "You-Your" were capitalized. The idioms of the Hebrew text were to be translated into equivalent English idioms: the difficult Hebrew coordinations and subordinations were to be expressed in more normal English. The intention was to reproduce the massoretic (or traditional) text faithfully, not trying to improve upon it, gloss over its difficulties or obscurities and not departing from it for esthetic or theological reasons. Possible emendations, ancient or modern, were indicated in the numerous footnotes. In effect, this is a scholarly translation which reads smoothly. The principal difficulty is the lingering desire to stay close to the King's English and to the traditional Hebrew text even when it can be safely improved.

Other Translations

Numerous other translations exist, some of them having enjoyed a brief popularity and some of them confined to professional circles. The King James Version has had several updatings such as the Revised Standard Version and New American Standard Bible of 1971. There are special purpose Bibles such as the Amplified Bible, the Holy Bible in the Language of Today, the Modern Language Bible. There are Bibles which had a short life span such as the Confraternity of Christian Doctrine Bible and Ronald Knox's Old and New Testament, or from an older age Edgar Goodspeed's Bible. The Anchor Bible series is a set of commentaries, usually on individual books, which includes a new critical translation of the text. This is not usable for our purposes in its present form, but it may have influence on the Bible translations of the future.

SELECTING A PURPOSE

Almost as important as picking a Bible is clarifying one's own purpose in reading it at all. You may use the Bible for any need, even the most pedestrian, and it will not object. But if you are interested enough to read a book about the Bible, you are ready also to clarify in your own mind just what you are doing this for. Plain curiosity is an honest enough reason for going deeper. It is perhaps disdainful to suggest that Bible reading is sometimes done simply to prove that someone's previous convictions were right. The Bible has surely been used for that and the word "used" takes on a different significance. Most people are much more open than that. We certainly do not read the Bible to undermine our previous faith commitment. Yet we are open to new insights, to an enrichment of what we have previously known, and eventually to letting the Bible take us where it will. In a few words, we are ready to listen and to profit. This book presumes that you are willing to do so.

It is observable that the scholars whom we must sometimes consult are subject to the same pressures, even if in a more subtle way. A favorite expression of the scholar begins: "If we are to avoid subjectivity. . . ." Objectivity may be avoided, though with great labor; subjectivity cannot be avoided. Arbitrariness surely should be avoided, but subjectivity should simply be acknowledged and kept in the subject, not pushed off on to the text. A simple example of this is the disposition of some scholars to speak of a "canon within the canon." If the phrase means no more than that some parts of the Bible affect us more deeply than others, it is an honest expression of our subjectivity. The minute descriptions of the boundaries of the tribes of Israel in the Book of Numbers, chapter 34, are not as important to us as the sayings of Jesus in Matthew, chapter 6 about living without anxiety. This is simply an inevitable judgment on what is useful to our lives. It is quite another thing to say that some parts of the Bible are not worth much in themselves. That transfers the judgment on usefulness from the reader to the Bible.

This has always been a problem in the history of Bible use. Marcion was a second-century shipowner who got interested in spreading a type of Christianity which would appeal. He cut out the entire Old Testament and most of the New Testament to eliminate the angry God whom he detected there. He provoked a great outcry from Christian writers who insisted that the Bible had to be taken as a whole. That tradition persists even in our English language; we speak of the Bible in the singular even though we know that there are many different books in it. As readers we shall need to take the book as a whole. If we find slavery spoken of as an accepted social condition, we cannot simply scissor out the passages. On a more touchy point, the Bible has a tendency to use sexist language. Some of this is due to the English translators who have unconsciously operated out of sexist prejudices; some of it is due to the changing condition of our language which gives diminishing value to "man" as a generic word and an increasing value to it as referring to males alone. But some of it is due to a heavy masculine hand in the Bible itself. To eliminate the sexist language from the Bible is to falsify the record. This is not to condone sexism or to try to give it biblical justification. It is simply to say that we must face the problem honestly.

The problem becomes more complex and central as the basic issues of religion are approached. The history of Christianity is full of violent arguments which still involve us. The question of "holy war" versus pacifism still exists and we may have strong emotional reactions on either side. Institutionalism in religion or a free spirit is a constant issue. Faith and works or any combination of the two defy consensus. This is not a book advocating any one religious approach to such problems. But the complications of our own deepest convictions and feelings must be faced. The danger of reading meaning into the Bible is ever present and I cannot presume that it has not crept into this book. It cannot be avoided; it should simply be recognized as honestly as we can do so. One need not agree with the Bible (and much less with this book). The only point being made is that there are things in the Bible which we shall probably dislike and that we disliked them before we read the Bible. If we read any authority into it at all, we cannot simply ignore our previous commitments or devise elaborate subterfuges for eliminating them from the book.

The contents of the Bible are themselves the bone of contention in the history of Jewish and Christian groups. Fortunately, we are drawing closer to a consensus on this point than we have for centuries. Christians of different sects have published ecumenical Bibles which contain the larger canon or list of sacred books. The disputed books are called either apocrypha or deuterocanonical. This book will occasionally quote from books which are only in the larger canon, such as Sirach or Wisdom.

If the book must be accepted as a whole, so must the people who wrote the various parts of it. Individually, they were a quite mixed bag, if we may judge from what they wrote. Holiness was not required to be a "sacred" author, although holiness in the sense of being a loyal believer was essential in having the writing accepted. Genius was not a requirement. An Isaiah or a Job or a Koheleth or a Ruth (to call authors by the names which their books bear) were geniuses and must stand high in the ranks of the all-time literary greats. Much of ben Sirach's book is pedestrian; Mark is rough and common. One cannot confine one's reading simply to those who were literary giants. The Obadiahs and the writers of the Pastoral Epistles must be taken along with the Hoseas and the Pauls, however lamentable we may think it to be. The people who wrote the Bible all belonged to one people and eventually all of them got together in one book.

There is one thing they all have in common; they were all Semites (except possibly Luke). Most of us are not, and that creates problems. At solving problems we are good; Semites are usually inefficient. At managing enterprises, they were incurably sloppy; we cannot live without clear lines of authority. They were endlessly children of the question; we of the answers. Above all, they were not systems people, but people people. They produced no great scientists or philosophers; they were not even very good at engineering and building, as archaeology attests. They could conquer, but not administer. Even Paul shows that trait. They wrote as the spirit moved, not as orderly composition dictated. In our kind of book, the pages follow one another with short groups of sentences set off from one another in paragraphs. We all learned how to write that way in school. There is little evidence that biblical authors wrote from an outline (although occasional works are intricately planned) or that they were much concerned with topic sentences in paragraphs. So also those who copied the books usually made no separation between words, sentences, and what we call paragraphs. Chapter and verse numbers are our invention, not theirs. The short outlines of biblical books which sometimes appear in introductory notes as we print the Bible, or which almost always appear in commentaries, are there to satisfy our needs, not theirs.

Consequently, we must be on our guard against overanalyzing their works. We want to get at the logic of each part and of the whole. Anyone who has ever tried the school-room exercise of diagraming one of Paul's sentences in the original Greek is apt to despair. The logical outlines given for any biblical work vary immensely from commentator to commentator. We feel a need, especially in this kind of book, to give and receive capsule summaries. "Tell me in a few words what the Gospel of John is all about." It is just as impossible to tell what John is all about in a few words as it is to condense one's best friend into a six-inch miniature.

We must not demand too much order or too much precision of our sort in the Bible. The central character of the book is God. He is never defined, proved, or diagnosed; he just exists. He comes on the scene dressed in anything from fire and thunder to a lover's robes. He is a good shepherd in a favorite Psalm and a warrior in the book of Revelation. He is pictured in a hundred ways and yet he is never confined to any one picture or even to all of them. So also the secondary characters. They are a kaleidoscope of characters. They are neither simple people nor primitive; they are just different. The models from which their literary artists drew their pictures are as sophisticated and complex as the writing itself. David is a most complex hero and antihero; Moses is a leader and yet not a leader; Jesus is a humble, commanding figure. Antitheses and paradox pervaded this people; they lived comfortably with contradictions. You must always suspect a sly twist in the most prosaic essays and a complication behind the simplest stories. A good deal of this book will be concerned with this problem.

The history of the formation of the Bible is itself a model of this complexity. It is apparent even to the casual reader that there are great varieties in the types of writing which the Bible contains. The books do not follow one another in a continuous chronological order either of story or of publication. Even the briefest introductions or footnotes will inform you that the work was written slowly over many centuries, edited, recast, and reinterpreted by many more authors than we can name even in the rare circumstance that we can name any of them. Yet somehow they all came to be together in one book.

A brief sampling of content and publication date of books as they appear in the Bible will illustrate the matter. We often do not know when they were originally written; we usually have more solid information as to when the final editing was done; hence, the "date of publication." The books cited here are those which we shall later use in some substantial way, not all of the books of the Bible. The order of commenting on them will be that found in the New American Bible, though any other translation would illustrate the same thing.

The Pentateuch (also called the Torah) is the name usually given to the collection named Genesis, Exodus, Leviticus, Numbers, and Deuteronomy. These books carry the early story of the Chosen People from the beginnings through the Exodus from Egypt to the end of the subsequent sojourn in the desert. They rely largely on oral traditions, some of great antiquity, but this material has been greatly expanded, edited, and reinterpreted from several different streams of tradition. The final work was put into the form we now have it some time before 400 B.C.

Joshua continues the story, telling of the conquest of the Promised Land. It relies loosely on ancient traditions from various cult places and has been re-edited several times. It probably reached its present form during the time of the Babylonian Exile (587–539 B.C.).

Judges is a somewhat disconnected series of very ancient stories which takes up after the time of Joshua. These stories are largely in their primitive form, but the arrangement and substantial editorial additions are probably from two later editors, the last of whom worked in the time of the Babylonian Exile.

Ruth is a story which was written as a story. If it was written close to actual events, it originated about 1100 B.C. and was probably published about 950 B.C.

1 and 2 Samuel tells the story of the tribes from about 1040 B.C. to the coming of the monarchy under David. These books contain incidents handed down by different (and sometimes differing) traditions, notably traditions concerning the monarchy. For our purpose, the so-called "Succession Narrative" which tells of the events leading up to the succession of Solomon to David (2 Samuel 8 to 1 Kings 2) is most important. This story was written probably during the times of Solomon (960–922 B.C.).

1 and 2 Kings continues the story of the kings of Judah and Israel from the time of Solomon to the Babylonian Exile. It contains court records, legends, stories, prophetic judgments, and other such material, all of which seems to have been put together during the Babylonian Exile. The whole complexus from Joshua to the end of 2 Kings is often called the Deuteronomist's history to indicate the dominant trend of thought which is first found in the Book of Deuteronomy and which seems to bind the whole together.

Judith is placed shortly after 2 Kings in most Bibles, but it was written some time during the second or first century B.C. It is an out-and-out fictional tale whose central character is called "the Jewess." It is not in the shorter canon.

Esther is a tale of derring-do by Babylonian Jews in escaping a pogrom. The Hebrew version probably dates to about 300 B.C.; the Greek translation which contains substantial additions dates to about a half century later. These additions are found only in some Bibles.

The Psalms (150 Psalms) were mainly songs used in Temple worship in Jerusalem. Their composition extends over many centuries from the beginning of the monarchy (about 1000 B.C.) to its end (587 B.C.) with a small number of Exilic and post-Exilic additions.

Proverbs is a long collection, mostly of individual wise sayings, some of extremely old vintage (such as the Sayings of Agur in Proverbs 30:1–6) and some grouped almost in essay form (cf. Proverbs 1–9) at a much later date in post-Exilic times.

Koheleth (sometimes spelled Qoheleth or translated as Ecclesiastes) is a much shorter collection of sayings, poems, and essay type reflections from a rather uncertain date, but most probably somewhere in the third or fourth century B.C.

Wisdom is a much later collection of such sayings although the continuous essay form is even stronger. It was written in Greek, presumably by an Alexandrian Jew some time between 100 and 50 B.C. It does not appear in the shorter canon.

Sirach also is an anthology of wise sayings but now prayers and poems are more to the front. It was written by a Palestinian Jew some time around 180 B.C. and later translated into Greek by the grandson of the author. It also does not appear in the shorter canon.

Isaiah introduces the prophetic books. This is a complex book which is usually broken down into three parts. The first thirty-nine chapters are mostly poems edited from the preaching of the first Isaiah which is dated circa 742–687 B.C. The preaching work seems to have been continued by various disciples. The second series of poems, called Deutero-Isaiah (chapters 40 to 54), seems to have been composed at the end of the Babylonian Exile and a third series, called Trito-Isaiah (chapters 55 to 66), apparently dates to the Persian period shortly thereafter.

Jeremiah is a much edited collection of sermons and poems by a prophet who preached between 628 and 587 B.C. or shortly thereafter and whose work was put in final form shortly after the Babylonian Exile.

Daniel, the next of the prophets, is a very late book of the type called apocalyptic. It was written some time during the persecution of the Jews by Antiochus IV Epiphanes (167–164 B.C.).

Hosea is a collection of sermons given by a Northern Israelite in the years before 746 B.C. or shortly thereafter.

Amos is from this same era and place, probably dated before 746 B.C. Some few passages may have been added later, but Amos is a carefully planned book and probably reflects the original author rather closely.

Jonah is listed among the minor prophets, but this book is really a short story with a deliberately comic twist. It was not a summary of preachings, as most of the other prophetic material, but a written work from the beginning. Its date is very uncertain, but probably fifth century B.C.

Habakkuk preached between 605 and 597 B.C. His brief collection of prophetic experiences, preachings, and canticles seems to have been published shortly thereafter.

Matthew is the first book to appear in the New Testament. It is a collection of stories about Jesus which has been considerably expanded by planned insertion of many sayings. It seems to have originated in Antioch between 80 and 100 A.D.

Mark is actually the earliest of the Gospels and the shortest, being composed mostly of stories about Jesus which were arranged and connected by editorial tie-ins to form the "gospel" style of writing. It probably dates to before 70 A.D.

Luke is the third account of the deeds and sayings of Jesus; it incorporates much of Matthew and Mark (and another common source), but adds its own incidents and recasts the whole story to make a different point. It was apparently written between 70 and 90 A.D.

John is different entirely from the other three Gospels which are called "synoptic" because they have much more of a common viewpoint. The Gospel of John apparently arose as various editions of sermons preached by disciples of John in Asia Minor were put together as a new interpretation of the deeds and sayings of Jesus. It probably reached its final form after several earlier editions by about 90 to 100 A.D.

Romans is Paul's most carefully planned treatise, an essay on wrath and redemption and the escape through faith into a life that could be lived in the Spirit. It was written about 52–56 A.D. before Paul had visited Rome.

1 Corinthians is an earlier letter of Paul's concerning problems which arose in the Christian community which Paul founded in Corinth. It dates to between 53 and 56 A.D.

Ephesians is a Pauline letter from somewhat later, but the dating is quite uncertain. If it stems directly from Paul, it was written in the early 60s; if it is from a disciple, it must be dated between 70 and 100 A.D.

This letter is really more of a prayer than an essay, a hymn of thanksgiving to God for the church and all that it meant in people's lives.

Revelation is the last book in the New Testament, a visionary tract similar to Daniel in apocalyptic style and intended to sustain Christians under persecution. It is usually dated between 90 and 100 A.D.

Many of these dates are only approximations; almost all of them are challenged by one scholar or another. Perhaps the most noteworthy suggestion is that of J.A.T. Robinson, who would move the dates of most of the New Testament books closer to the beginnings and date none of the books later than about 75 A.D.

Despite all the uncertainties, several things are clear from this or any other plausible list of dates of publication. First of all, there was usually a considerable length of time between the events and the final edition of the writing about them. This is especially true of the so-called "historical" writing. The time between is filled in with "oral tradition"; obviously, the time lapse was much longer in Old Testament writing than in the New Testament. Sufficient study has been made of oral tradition in other cultures and literatures to confirm that stories can indeed be carried in substantially the same form over centuries by oral retelling. Names of places and people in particular have an intense durability. Second, it should be noted that there are high points of intense literary activity. The first occurs about 1000 B.C. during the time of David and Solomon. The period during the Babylonian Exile and shortly thereafter is also a time of high activity. The fifties of the first Christian century mark a high point as the Pauline writings begin to appear, and the late sixties and seventies seem to have marked another period of Gospel and Epistle writing (unless one adopts a later chronology which would shift this to the eighties and later). More often than not, these high points are associated with times of innovation or stress—the new monarchy of Davidic-Solomonic times, the Babylonian Exile, the persecution of the Seleucids, the new Christian enterprise, and the inception of trials both within and without the community. The third peculiarity to note is that the reflective materials in the Old Testament seem to have been written rather late in the development, whereas in the New Testament this was the first thing to be consigned to writing. The Epistles take for granted that the readers are familiar with the oral tradition of the stories and do not repeat it; they comment upon it for insights into the meaning of those stories. Finally, it should be noted that the New Testament has no prophetic books as such. The final book called Revelation is not really a "prophecy"; it is a type of writing called apocalyptic which falls somewhere between wise reflection on history and projection.

Scholarly research has uncovered even more complexities in the history than this very brief survey indicates. Some understanding of the present state of that scholarly effort is needed if one is to read not only the Bible but the mainline commentators, whether or not one agrees with them. For example, it will be taken for granted here that the Gospel of Matthew was not written by one author at one time. Before Matthew there were sayings of the Lord which had already come into some fairly definite form. Then there were stories—miracles stories, conflict stories, stories which led to some sort of punch line. Yet these were not frozen into solid form. The Passion Story seems to have been the earliest section of the narrative of Jesus which came together and it is fairly consistent in all four Gospels. The Resurrection Stories, on the other hand, seem to have had but little standard form and so the four Gospels have very different ways of telling them. If we compare Matthew to Mark and Luke, we can detect not only the common elements and the distinctive material, but also the editorial comments and arrangements of the whole work. In technical terms the process of diagnosing the form and history of the individual units in the Gospels is called Form Criticism (or better, the history of the forms); the process of diagnosing how the final editor put the parts together and the point being made is called Redaction Criticism.

It is also helpful to know something of what happened to the Bible after it was finally accepted as sacred scripture. As the Bible had a strong tendency to reinterpret earlier writings in the light of new situations, so also the writers of succeeding ages continued to reinterpret the Bible in the light of their own situations. Historians of the subject can outline great movements in interpretation which sometimes lasted for centuries. Then society changed and new ways of interpreting the Bible arose. That a more scientific approach to understanding the Bible has appealed to many of our age is understandable since interpretation follows need. Yet each age has left its impact and residue. Most of what we write about the Bible today is either an attempt to meet our needs with new approaches or, in rejection, to go back to older ways. The realization that every age has tried to make the Bible relevant without ever reaching a final and definitive statement of what the Bible means in all its fullness should warn us that our present approaches are probably as transient as those of any earlier age. On the other hand, it is also comforting to know that we do not need to reach the one and only final conclusion either.

At the end of this section let us return to the beginning. With all of the complexities, both within the Bible and within ourselves, we can still look at the literature in the Bible and accept it as one book. It is published that way and the centuries have accepted it in that way. We may like one author better than another; we may like satisfying one of our personal needs more than another. But if we are to be honest (and among the honest convictions is probably that the Bible is special and in some way the Word of God), then we must accept it as a whole and have as a purpose the understanding of the Bible as a whole. We throw out a little bit of God every time we reject some part of the Bible.

GETTING ACQUAINTED WITH THE BIBLE AND OURSELVES

It takes two to get acquainted. If the Bible is like a living person, then we ourselves are the other part of the relationship. This takes some untangling. There is obviously a way to read the Bible mechanically—we may hear too much of that in church. We may do it ourselves, letting the words slip by before our eyes without ever being struck with the thought. Familiar texts, like familiarity in other areas, breed contempt or at least unthinking tolerance. So we must get into a reflective mood in order to listen.

The advocates of the New Hermeneutic have invented a sentence which says: the text interprets the reader. This is, of course, deliberately provocative. It is a good provocation if it makes us advert to what happens whenever we read anything. If we read the daily paper, we all have different reactions—annoyance, anger, despair, elation, humor, fear, and so on. We express it in our words, our gestures, and our facial expressions. If we tell what is in the newspaper, we do not simply repeat the words. We tell our reaction to the story. The text has brought out of us something of what we are, something of what we stand for. Somebody else knows where we stand. The text has interpreted the reader in the sense that it has forced us to reveal something of ourselves.

Even private reading does that. We say we are struck by something we have just read. Something has leaped out of the page even though we may have read it many times before. It is not a totally new thought which has come to us, but in some way it unites a lot of thinking which we have done before. It gives us something of a center of unity at least for a while, and we may live on one of those bright thoughts for days or years. We know ourselves better for having read what someone else wrote. The text has interpreted us to ourselves. This is not to say that the words mean something different at different times or to different individuals. It is not a relapse into terminal subjectivism, but it recognizes the fact of experience that the message of words affects each of us in a somewhat different way. We give more importance to this or that thought than someone else does, to this or that phrase which strikes us as being precisely right. We organize what we have read in different ways. Any preacher knows that after the sermon there will probably be as many different understandings of what he or she has said as there are people in the audience. We cannot explain the difference on the basis of the word; that is the same for all. The difference is in the interpretative process which goes on within us.

DECIDING HOW DEEPLY YOU WANT TO GET INTO THIS

It would be well at this point to be a bit afraid. If the text interprets the reader, we may not be all that anxious to have ourselves interpreted to ourselves. We may want to go back to the earlier level of sheer curiosity. Yet even that decision interprets ourselves. So it may be time for us to examine our own decision-making.

Do you want to continue reading this book? You now know the tack that it will take. It may not be to your liking or beliefs or convictions or tastes. Such reactions need no justification except to yourself. Since you have already invested this much time, it might be worthwhile for you to pinpoint precisely why you did not like the first chapter. The process of doubling back to observe ourselves doing what we do is one of the more valuable human occupations. Where did the process of decision-making start? Did it start with a judgment on style? Or on evidence? Or on prejudgments? If you have gotten this far, you must have made some positive judgments to get here. On what basis did you make those judgments? What have you learned from the experience? How do you see yourself now? Just knowing that much will give you some reward for coming this far.

On the other hand, if you think that you will continue reading, what can you expect to get into? The rest of this book will presume that you will have a Bible at hand and will do some reading around the various examples that are used. You may already know some of these stories if you are a Bible reader. Others you will need to look up. The book will also presume that you are willing to listen to what the mainline of scholarly research is saying about the Bible. This is not a scholarly book; it will not demand that minute attention to details and to the accumulation of scientific papers without which the professional scholar or student feels uncomfortable. Yet it will leave the door open to further study of that sort if you want to go that way.

At the end of this book is a bibliography for those who are interested in a more scholarly approach. The bibliography presumes that you already are or are becoming familiar with the general field of biblical research. The books and articles listed are those which bear on the peculiar approach this book takes and which I found most useful in writing it. If you read some or all of them, you shall be retracing some of the steps which I took. Much more has been written and should be noted in a complete bibliography. How much more I do not know. The field is enormous. One always hopes that a dialogue will begin among scholars, but that high ideal is not frequently realized. At best we seem to talk to ourselves and not to the people who will really be the users and final judges of what we have done. Appealing to the general reader is often of more value for all concerned.

The approach I am taking does diverge from the mainline scholarly research in its appeal to experience, especially the experience of literature. That too is open-ended. You can confront experience simply by reading this book privately and measuring what has been said against your own experience of life. This book presumes that you will do so. The Epistle to Timothy urged reading of the Bible since "all scripture is useful. . . ." (2 Timothy 3:16) If it is not useful, it should not be read. If it is read, then it must come into immediate use in judging one's own experience. But the test of what is truly useful has always been whether it is useful for the whole community of believers—in this case, even the community of believers in literature. That is why the Bible has been preserved and that is the only way in which it has and can function as a document affecting society. Much of the material originated as oral tradition—people told one another what the ancient beliefs were and in the telling subtly modified them as they made them confront their present needs. Some of it was written for public worship in which people sung or said to one another what they really believed. Such are the Psalms of the Old Testament and the various liturgical hymns in the New Testament. Even after the text was finalized, the discussion went on. The Epistles were meant to be read publicly; there are evidences that prior epistles had been discussed, argued over, and rejected. We must presume that the final Epistle was treated in the same way. Then they came to be the subject of sermons, essays, and poems. The same thing happened to the Gospels. In later centuries the Gospels were communicated not only by the text but also by sermons, tracts, paintings, stained glass windows ("the cathedrals were the Bible of the poor"), plays, and all those numerous other ways in which people communicate with one another. The Bible was never intended to be a secret book; it arose out of the people, was by the people, and for the people. To savor its full meaning is to bring it out today into discussion with others so that experience may be measured against experience.

A second bibliography is provided for you if you want to venture into this field. All over the country groups of people assemble to study the Bible. The range is from formal academic classes to unstructured and occasional discussions which we have on the spur of the moment. Bible study may denote anything from discussion structured around printed material and audio-visual aids to prayer meetings in which none of these props are used. The bibliography makes references to sources which can supply good materials. All of the major church groups have such publications; the bibliography makes no pretense of covering them all. You may find that your own church organization has more suitable materials. At least, you should inquire. But perhaps the best suggestion is not to be found in the bibliography at all. Why don't you just join a Bible study group of some sort and discover whether you like it? An appendix at the end of this book gives suggestions on how to organize a Bible Study Group.

TWO

Reading the Bible as Literature

THE PROBLEM OF PROFESSIONAL SCHOLARS

Biblical scholars have a crisis on their hands. For a century they have been perfecting new tools to diagnose the Scriptures. The current interest in the Bible is evidence enough that they have succeeded very well in making the Bible more intelligible and engaging. Yet the profession is beset today with an honest wonderment: is that all there is? It is the scholars themselves who are doing the criticizing. One must respect their honesty and profit from their analysis before venturing too far into a field which they have largely created and which must necessarily depend so much upon their learning.

The problem seems to center on the fascination with the tools of the trade rather than on the living Word. It is perhaps most clear if we consider the field of archaeology. Archaeological discoveries, such as those at Qumran, or more recently at Ebla, make headlines. There are pictures to see, romantic tales to be told, scientific evidence such as radiocarbon dating to be cited. All of this gives a feeling of solid evidence for the scholar as well as for the general reader. This is the kind of material at which we are competent as no earlier age was competent. We are at home with it and without being aware of what we are doing, we interpret it to satisfy our needs. Science and objectivity are familiar grounds which we claim. The Bible, however, was not written to be scientific and objective; it was written to be human and to affect human subjects. Both archaeology and the Bible have interpretative elements in them, but they are not running on the same track.

Archaeology is only one example and, indeed, biblical archaeology is only one branch of a much larger discipline. Archaeologists are digging up previous cultures all over the world. Some of the material is epigraphic; that is, inscribed. We now know a great deal about the ancient peoples, from their tax records to their myths about the gods. The religious elements dominate in archaeology. The most important buildings that the previous ages constructed, whether simple *kivas* in the American Southwest or the pyramids of Egypt, had a religious purpose. Sculptures, inscriptions, ornaments, burial sites, and a host of other things attest to religious ideas and practices. So we have built up a vast warehouse of information on religious beliefs of the past and we can compare them with one another. Thus comparative religion enters the field of biblical study. This, too, is a scientific study which satisfies our feeling that we have put our hands on something which proves this or that. The almost necessary temptation, therefore, is to find more of this and that both to unearth and to prove.

Archaeology, however, is but a small part of the picture of how the fascination with the tools of the trade affect us. I am going to draw a picture of the progress of the biblical sciences in modern times. You will understand that it is something of a caricature since it is painted with a broad brush. But the picture is needed if something of the present crisis is to be understood.

The earlier study of the Bible often concentrated on the question: How was this book written? Since there was little external evidence, the diagnosis had to proceed from within. It was assumed, for instance, that Moses had written the Pentateuch, that Joshua had written the book called by his name, that David had written most of the Psalms, that the Book of Proverbs was at least in part written by Solomon, that Matthew had written his Gospel from what he had personally witnessed, and so on. It was also assumed as a dictate of faith that in some way the book had been "dictated" from on high, whatever that expression meant and sometimes it meant virtually a mechanical process. The scientific age demanded a different answer. It was especially the German historicists who began to apply the diagnostic tools of history to the Bible. Rules of evidence were applied to the Bible as they were to other historical documents. Truth was to be found in the accuracy of descriptions as they matched the facts. Various forms of ancient writing were recognized, such as myths, etiological stories (that is, narratives about the origin of a name), court records, and so forth, and sifted to discover what had actually happened. This is a delicate procedure since it can get at factuality only indirectly. For example, the excavations at Jericho seem to confirm the story which the Bible tells of its destruction. There are burnt walls and storehouses with scorched grain; the foundations are bent by some enormous force, presumably an earthquake. Unfortunately, the data from Jericho and other sites also indicate that in the period of destruction there were no Hebrews around. The method of historical criticism could often cast doubt on whether the biblical accounts were factual, but could not solve the problems.

Meanwhile, the literary analysis of the biblical material into forms of writing indicated that much of the writing was a compilation from earlier sources. The previous listing of dates of publication of some of the books gives evidence of this. The historian was interested in this study since the investigation of history demands that sources of information be evaluated. Instead of having evidence that one person was the source of the material in each book, it became clear that most books contained very divergent styles, vocabulary, and viewpoints. The Bible contains numerous duplications; the extent and consistency of the divergences argues that there were different sources. So today professional scholars speak of at least four principal sources underlying the Pentateuch and numerous others in the so-called "historical" books. The same process can be seen in the Synoptic Gospels. It is clear that there is a common source (called Q for *quellen*, the German for "source") behind much of Matthew, Mark, and Luke. There are also differences, but the differences are found mostly in the introductions or conclusions or in the arrangements of materials. It is as though the material originally had a certain form and later developed into the present text.

When the separation of biblical materials into units of literary forms is combined with a study of sources and the history of the development of the sources, we have Form Criticism, or to be more true to the original German meaning, "the history of the forms." The term is used in New Testament study, but is equally applicable with some changes to Old Testament research.

Once these tools of scholarship were forged and honed, the trend of later research was to refine them and to apply them more and more precisely. So more theories arose which demanded more forms and this led to more research to discover more parallels in cognate literatures. Archaeology and its cognate fields of philology and epigraphy (or manuscript study) aided the process. In effect, the biblical exegete or interpreter was following much the same procedure as the archaeologist. The archaeologist excavates a *tell* or mound by removing or penetrating through layer after layer from the top down. The parallel was sufficiently strong to label the exegete's method "the scientific method."

At this point—and the point is now—it seems to many scholars that what we have on the dissecting table is a corpse. The doctor is not smiling. The living Word has ceased to be living. It is somewhat of a caricature, to be sure, but it has enough truth to strike home. Let it be said for the doctors that they were the ones to recognize the signs of *rigor mortis*. You have already rubbed shoulders with some of them in this book and you will need to understand more about them in what follows. The patient should know something about how the doctor feels.

In their own analysis of the problem the experts cite the following as some of the major symptoms of the crisis. First, a rigidity of seeking literary genres and forms has set in which no longer reflects the free flow of writing which makes literature alive. Our canons of writing have become so precise that we over-analyze and demand of the author a conformity to ways of writing which we cannot prove he knew are too rigid. Literary forms do not often occur with the purity which we postulate. We have forgotten that we created these forms to satisfy our own needs. Second, we have virtually eliminated any way of getting at historical fact in our attempt to dictate the way in which history should be written. To cite the most important example, the historical Jesus has vanished behind a history of the forms and sources in which his story was told. Third, we have become so enamoured of our search for sources (Samuel Sandmel once called it "parallelomania") that we tend to tie together a chain of probabilities and suppositions from morphological data, cognate literatures, theological themes, living situation of the author, and so on, and call it a conclusion when it is only an educated guess. Finally, the sport of finding new sources and more and more minute forms has led us into an antiquarianism which no longer seems to have much relevance. We are in danger of being frozen in the sea of historical criticism.

It is no wonder that some people have reacted in the opposite direction and have insisted that we should simply go back to the fundamental that the Bible is the revealed word of God and that we should not bother much about all of these human factors which may have led to its production. This approach is called Fundamentalism, although the word covers a vast diversity of variations.

In this book we shall try to look at the Bible in a somewhat different way; namely, as literature. What do we mean by literature? How is it different from other writing? Although we sometimes say that we picked up some "literature" from a car dealer or at a political rally, we know that this is not the central meaning of the word. Nor is a textbook on chemistry, however good a textbook it may be, considered as literature. Nor is a textbook on theology. Nor is a book on how to repair one's automobile. Nor is a legal brief. There are many things which are not literature. So what defines true literature? The dictionary, which records our use of words, states that literature is "writings in which expression and form, in connection with ideas of permanent and universal interest are characteristic or essential features." Both the permanence and the universal interest are of importance to us.

The subject here is not the "oohs" and "aahs" of biblical literature. There are plenty of beautiful passages in the Bible; indeed, some of our finest word craftsmanship is to be found here. But this is not the point. Let us look first at the permanence. The Bible is part of our enduring record of life on the planet and no further reference need be made to its staying power. However, there are many other pieces of writing which were also intended as permanent records, for example, credal statements, constitutions, confessions, and proclamations, serious theological books which have endured the test of centuries. Yet we would hardly classify them as "literature" despite their permanence. The Bible has permanence precisely as literature, and we miss a good deal if we do not view it in that way. We must look at the way literature is intended to function.

When you go to a store, you get a piece of paper with words and numbers printed on it. It functions as a receipt for you and probably as an inventory for the store. It is different from your shopping list. Neither will function very well as a greeting card. A legal summons looks different from a sales ticket; it is couched in odd language and it accomplishes something else. A death notice in a newspaper has a certain format about it; it functions precisely as a notice. It is not a panegyric nor a condolence card. In short, writing occurs in a variety of forms which have different functions. The functions in turn are dictated by the needs of the society which is functioning.

The first thing to note then is that the Bible functioned as a record of the experience of the people who felt mysteriously that they had been chosen by a God to keep alive true knowledge and worship. The record was intended to be permanent and it became so. The great body of English literature is taught year after year in our schools and read with pleasure by many people. Nobody has passed a law which says that this is the body of English literature or that it must be preserved. It simply has too much to say to all of us about our roots to be ignored. Time and culture are bridged in great literature; it is a living thing whose life is its own, not subject to our passing fads and minor crises. Some of it appeals more to us in one age than in another; but the great writings recycle themselves for another need at a later time. It is permanent, but in a very dynamic way.

In our tradition about the Bible we call this process of "permanentizing" canonicity. Nobody in Old Testament times ever decreed that such and such books belonged to the Bible. They were simply accepted by the people on their worth. Nor did any of the New Testament writers decree that their writings should be permanent. It took several centuries before Church authority made any efforts in this direction and the final "canonizing" was not formally done until the sixteenth century. There was always some doubt about a few books which appeared toward the end of either Old Testament or New Testament times (seven in each Testament) and so in the Christian tradition we have both a shorter and a longer canon. This is no longer considered a serious problem; the shorter contains all the essentials and the longer represents authentic Old and New Testament reflection on the events in the record. What is quite evident is that there simply arose out of popular acceptance that a certain group of books, whatever the precise listing, and those only do form the permanent record of Judaism and Christianity.

In addition to the permanence, we must also note the universal appeal. On almost every page it pictures with remarkable lifelikeness the men and women who wanted to know more about how God was involved in their wars and protests, in their longings and expectations, in their defeats and victories. They wanted to have insight into all of these things; they struggled and sometimes succeeded superbly in saying the exact words which alone could express their thoughts. They did not always succeed; sometimes their literature fell far below that benchmark that we set up for such noble writing. But in the totality of the Bible, this, too, was necessary and established the reality of the human condition out of which they worked. They were not often theorists or abstract thinkers. They dealt with concrete circumstances through preference and they expressed themselves more naturally in images than in propositions. Those images were often so universal in appeal that the second requirement of literature was met. But more must be said about this in some detail.

THE IMAGES OF LITERATURE

First, it should be noted that we actually have several different kinds of language. There is our common language, whether spoken or written. It is used easily, often without much attention to precisely how we say things. That differs from person to person, of course, since some people always strive to say precisely what they mean and some just babble on. Perhaps that is the tipoff as to how common language functions. We use it for all sorts of prosaic things such as to report facts ("It's raining"), or to give commands ("Pick up the papers"), or to express opinions ("Joe Smith doesn't have a leg to stand on"), and so on. But underneath all of this we are revealing ourselves. Common language reveals who we are at this precise moment. It is not a statement to be carved on stone. It passes with the moment and the next revelation of ourselves in common language may be completely different.

Technical language is quite different. When a doctor diagnoses the patient's condition and says "myocardial infarction," he is not saying very much about himself. He is using a term which has had a precise and standard meaning in the medical textbooks for a long time. It is understood all over the medical world. It is connected with a system of diagnosis and treatment which is standard and impersonal. Lawyers also use formalized language of this sort. The sentences may seem convoluted to the layman, but the expressions are formulas which have been developed over the years for the sake of precision and compactness. Nor is the practice restricted to such upper echelon professions; automobile mechanics have their own vocabulary; even checkout clerks have a code with which to call their supervisors.

Finally, there is literary language. It develops from common language and always retains the feature of personal revelation. Yet the pictures it paints are larger than the individual. The picture fits a great variety of individuals without becoming a "principle" or an abstraction. It is both a mirror in which one looks at one's self and a window through which one looks out on the world. Because it captures a broad spectrum of human experience, it tends to be universal and can easily become permanent. Although literary language develops before technical language, it already has some of the precision of technical language. The literary artist, like the scientist, must name reality precisely. There is one word, and only one word, which captures the idea with all the nuances and suggestiveness which is desired. Also, like technical language, literary language tends to become somewhat removed from common language. The difference may be ever so slight; the literary style may retain the most picturesque and direct sayings of common speech. On the other hand, it may become so formal and stylized that it has lost its contact and force and becomes sheer pretentiousness. As it approaches this point, it must turn back to recover its vitality and regain its touch with the living speech.

Now if the Bible is looked at as literature, we become aware that we must take a certain stance toward it. It, too, will speak largely in images. In the beginning it tells a story of the creation of all things. At first we might imagine that it is making technical statements about various things which were created and that these statements are impersonally transferable to other areas such as astronomy or botany or zoology or comparative religion or theology. However, when the whole composition is taken for what it is, we become aware that we are being involved with pictures which are drawn before our eyes. As we watch an exuberantly creative God make and people a whole world, we find ourselves watching him as he makes one final image of himself and that image is us. But that merely leads up to the final scene in the story, the seventh day, and on that day God does nothing. The author has done what the good literary artist should do; he (we presume) has created an unforgettable drama in pictures. But he has done more than use a clever technique; his composition rings with honest conviction that he has captured a reality not just in words, but in ourselves. As we watch the pictures being drawn, we find that a response is demanded from us. It may be awe; it may be rejection; it may be that we are struck with the enormous absurdity that this warring, thieving, whoring, deceiving race of humans is made in the image of God. Or must we change our image of God? The image offers no final solution. It is open-ended; it engages our experience of life; it is dynamic in that it goes on creating more images.

The rest of this book shall consider how the Bible, as literature, uses images in a great variety of ways. The stories, the parables, the sermons of the prophets, the reflections of the wise men, the pictures of the age to come, the interpretations of past events all tend to be expressed in images which arise out of experience. They do not often arise out of abstract technical language and we are the more to be pitied for trying to make them emerge in that way. For example, we try to make what is said about wisdom in Proverbs 1–9 emerge from a scientific search among pagan sources for some emanation from God that was usually called a goddess of wisdom. We have the theory first and then we hang on to it names which we know were given to various statues or which appear in ancient texts. The abstraction comes first. So we conclude that Lady Wisdom in the Bible (cf. Proverbs 9) or the Word (cf. John 1:1–18) is first of all an abstraction and only later a definite person. But both from a literary and an ancient Near Eastern point of view, it makes better sense to say that the first experience was of a woman or a definite man and then by looking deeply into that real person an area of mystery which said something of an image of God was detected. The image was not literary clothing; it already existed in the reality of the persons. It vanished finally into mystery, but that is where true artistry always vanishes and where the true understanding of reality hides itself. It is not really our scientific way of doing things on a professional level. But that is what the poets and artists do. It is very often what we do in common speech except that we don't think about it. It takes a bit of reflection to analyze our way of thinking, but the heightening of our awareness of this is well worth the effort.

THE INTERPRETATION OF EXPERIENCE

Whether we realize it or not, we are always interpreting any bit of writing out of our own experience. So, also, the biblical writing is not a thing, but a living word. The people who wrote it, wrote it from experience, often very crucial. Many times their lives hung on what they said; some of them died for writing it. More often, they realized that their lives were going to be changed by what they wrote. They had gone through the experience before they expected their readers to follow them. Those readers had their own experiences. The two either rubbed shoulders or butted heads. In no way could the text simply pass before their eyes.

The same happens to us. Our experience comes into play as soon as we read what some unknown Psalmist once wrote:

That you love me I know by this,
  that my enemy does not triumph over me.
                                Psalm 41:12

We may savor our memories of triumph and find it very satisfactory.
We may react by saying: "I know what that means, but I don't like
myself to feel like that." One way or another we have experienced the
situation. We may savor with more lightness of heart the saying of
the proverb writer who noted:

"Bad, bad!" says the buyer;
  but once he has gone his way, he boasts.
                                Proverbs 20:14

We have all had that experience or heard it as a boast from others. It
may strike us as childish or shrewd or comical, but we know what the
saying means. And we make our judgments.

The examples given above are very simple and superficial. They
are proverbial in nature, and proverbs are basically observations of how
people act. However, much of the Bible is written from this viewpoint
and we make a large mistake when we complicate it with principles
and technical language instead of seeing it as experience and common
language. A good sample of more substantive observation is found in
Romans 7:7–8:1. This is a famous passage about Paul's internal struggle.

I should never have known what evil desire was unless the law had said,
"You shall not covet." Sin seized that opportunity; it used the commandment to rouse in me every kind of evil desire. . . . We know that
the law is spiritual, whereas I am weak flesh sold into the slavery of sin.
I cannot even understand my own actions.
                                Romans 7:7–8 and 14–15

Who is involved in this struggle? The language of science would
say: *Man.* Man is then analyzed on various models of Greek and other
thought, and many parallels are adduced in secular writing of the time.

Or one grafts on to the passage a contemporary terminology of psychology or philosophy. A more traditional approach is to conclude, out of previous piety, that since the Apostle Paul was a saint, he must have been describing the trials he had before he was converted. This in turn may lead to confirming an already formed theology of the kind of person we all were before conversion and so on into various theologies of what "original sin" actually is. All of this is rather heady and certainly beyond what the literature was saying, whether the later theorizing is right or wrong.

The odd thing is that most people who have had enough experience of life to have suffered some real victories and defeats and to have come to grips with themselves honestly are apt to understand what Paul was talking about without all this theorizing. They need the help of some scientific aids, mostly to assure them that they are on the right track. They need to be told that the literary form does indeed arise out of a reflection on personal experience, that the passage begins and ends as noted at Romans 7:7 and 8:1, that the "law" is both the Mosaic Law which Paul learned as a boy and anything else that can be designated as law, and that by "flesh" he simply refers to himself in one area of his conduct. With this in mind the passage becomes a story which Paul tells about himself. He remembers his boyhood and how easy it was to recite those commandments. It did not cost much to memorize: "You shall not covet." But then he did and law wore a different face. That struggle goes on within him to the present day. Yet alongside of it is the experience of salvation. The ending says it all.

> "My inner self agrees with the law of God, but I see in my body's members another law at war with the law of my mind; this makes me a prisoner of the law of sin in my members. What a wretched man I am! Who can free me from this body under the power of death? All praise to God, through Jesus Christ our Lord! So with my mind I serve the law of God but with my flesh the law of sin. There is no condemnation now for those who are in Christ Jesus."
>
> Romans 7:22–8:1

You need not have recourse to weighty tomes or theological systems to understand this. If you have had the experience, you know what Paul is talking about. If you have not had it, or are unwilling to admit it within your secret room, then no amount of theorizing will make the passage come alive. How you will judge what this means is another thing. How it shall be fitted into a system of theology or a confession of faith is the work of later generations. That is not the point of this book. The only point of approaching the Bible as literature is to realize the significance of looking at your own experiences and being aware that you are already making a judgment on the basis of comparing Paul's experiences with your own.

The role of concrete experience in our lives and in the literary portrayal of it must be carefully assessed. We make decisions mostly on the basis of images. It is not that we "imagine" things—that, indeed, may happen and lead us astray from the beginning. We try to be sensible about facing facts. But our decisions are not made on facts; they are made on the way in which we see ourselves within the facts. This is "imaging." The literary author also uses images to represent the real crises in which we live. Without the ability to communicate through images and to stir up imagination, the literary author is handcuffed. The technician may indeed communicate in impersonal language, but such an author does not produce literature.

In reading the Bible you ought to begin by picturing what is going on. The genius of the people who wrote the Bible was to see concrete events and to picture them even when they seem to be talking to us in the propositional language of technicians. Imagination is the magic ingredient; it may also be the deadliest poison. Plato wanted to banish all poets from his ideal Republic for he feared that the imagination of poets could not be controlled. Indeed this is a danger. All through history people have read the Bible, imagined that they were present at the scene, and so reached conclusions. It was often totally subjective and led to bloodcurdling conclusions; it was an exercise of seeing their own images rather than the biblical ones. In daily life we know that this is self-deception; we must keep in contact with the facts even though they do not determine our decisions by themselves. So in biblical reading we must be willing to face the facts insofar as the science of scholarship can define them for us. We must use, for example, archaeology to describe scenes as accurately as possible. There is no sense, for example, in placing Jesus in grandiose scenes when the sheer logistics of population, wealth, architecture, and language will not allow us to do so. There is no sense in interpreting a wise observation as a law or a story as factual history if the study of literary forms tells us that this is not what was really happening. Various sciences establish controls over the way in which we use imagination.

On the other hand, we must not get lost in a fruitless quest for objectivity. It has been the rallying cry of scholarship for the past hundred years since it appeals to our scientific mentality. What is objectivity is itself a subjective decision. For some it means objective history or factual record; for others it means verbal objectivity insofar as our translations and explanations exactly equal the original sayings; for others it means theological objectivity (although most theologians know that they operate on faith and not on provable conclusions). How much it can be achieved is another subjective decision. For some any scholarship which is not endlessly verified by footnotes and specific data is no scholarship at all; for others it is the data which must be precise although the conclusions are the creation of the subject who is doing the writing. We prize today the tools that biblical scholarship has developed over the past century. There is no doubt that we can name the tools and tell how they should be used. But that they are the only tools available, and that such and such tools should be used on this particular problem, is a subjective decision based largely on the appeal which such things make to our own culture and to the individual exegete. Other ages and other cultures and other exegetes have found life satisfactory without them.

What is clear is that imagination must be allowed its legitimate play, but not allowed to run riot. We are reading literature and literature demands that we exercise imagination. If the scientist can help us to recognize a story as a story, and indeed a particular kind of story such as a parable, then he must also recognize that the interpretation of the story will largely depend on the imagination of the reader. Imagination is open-ended, as are images. There is no absolute way of saying that this is what the story means and only this. Later in this book we shall be analyzing stories. Let it be understood that the analysis is an aid to your own imagination. It is intended to plot a direction in which the story goes, not to mark off once and for all where the story ends. Fortunately, scholars themselves are becoming aware of this, especially in describing parables. Instead of looking at parables as simple exemplar stories which give us a model for action, we are now prepared to admit that they are rather mysterious and more often leave us with a question than with an answer.

The point being made is simply one that concerns literature. If you read the Bible as literature, you must take into account the whole sweep of the passages which you read. They were written out of an author's experience. They must be interpreted as a whole experience inasmuch as they reveal a person. So also the reading discloses your self. Some sort of equation will need to be made to accommodate yourself to the trajectory that seems to be forming in the biblical reading. The trajectory may say something important about your own longings or expectations. The future and the possible may disclose something of your present and of your hopes. As literature the Bible elevates to a higher level than we are accustomed to tread. All great literature does that, but the Bible is the best source of tried and true great literature. It lives.

THREE

How to Read Stories in the Bible

LOCATING THE STORY

A great part of the Bible is in the story form. The book begins with a story about creation and ends with an odd tale of cosmic struggle in the skies. In between, kings and priests, prophets and preachers of all kinds, loyal friends and implacable enemies, heroines and villains rub shoulders and contend with one another. Some of the stories we instinctively label as "history" and others as "story." The Passion Narrative sounds factual to us and we take it to be history; the parables we recognize as made-up stories. It may seem to be going back to our childhood to emphasize the story element, but scholars today are beginning to do this very thing. However, before we get involved in their technicalities, we should clarify some of our own ideas about story.

Story is the easiest form of writing or speaking to recognize. The account may include official records, poetry, long speeches expressing opinions, or elaborate descriptions, but we still recognize it as a story. It is also easier to identify a good story than a good poem or a good essay. Oddly, there is a kind of logic in storytelling that is more obvious and demanding than in other forms of speech. Any public speaker knows that a rigidly developed line of logic may be lost on the audience.

But let the speaker forget one crucial detail in a story and everybody in the audience will know it immediately. Unity is absolutely essential for good storytelling.

To have unity we must know where a story begins and ends. In the Bible this is not always easy; sometimes it is extremely difficult. A mild example is the beginning of the Bible. Genesis 1:1–2:4 tells the story of the seven days of creation and Genesis 2:5–3:24 continues with the story of the Garden of Eden. These are two entirely separate stories; they have different authors, different styles, were written centuries apart, and make quite different points. We know this from a sophisticated technique of diagnosis of literary forms and sources. Yet the scholar also knows that the final editor did use both stories together to describe some understandings of how life on this earth began. The ordinary reader is more apt to read the two stories together. Some rather complex things are happening here.

Some indications are found in biblical narratives which alert us to the fact that a new story is beginning. The ancients did not space out paragraphs or stories visually; the text all ran together. Chapters and verses, which help us, are a very late invention of medieval times. So there was need to include in the text certain phrases which set off the beginning and ending of a passage. In the Gospels we often have geographical or chronological indications for the beginning of a new story: "Leaving so-and-so, he went to. . . .", or "After this Jesus said. . . ." In the Book of Judges the stories begin with "The Israelites did what was evil in the sight of God" and conclude with "The land was calm." The story is neatly wrapped between the phrases. A similar device, used largely in late Old Testament instructions and in some of the New Testament, is called inclusion. A key word is used at the beginning of a passage and repeated at the end. A parallel technique is used by Mark and called the "envelope technique." A story begins with some fact or incident which does not seem to be highly important at first sight, but comes in later to signal the conclusion. For example, the story in Mark 3:20–35 begins with Jesus entering the house and there his family comes to get him. It ends in Mark 3:35 with Jesus saying "Whoever does the will of God is brother and sister and mother to me." In between the story concerns the quite different matter of the accusation by the scribes that Jesus had a devil. The whole incident is neatly packaged by the reference to the family.

So the first requirement for reading a biblical story is to mark off the beginning and the ending. Aristotle made a comment about that centuries ago which may seem simplistic but is absolutely basic: a story must have a beginning, a middle and an end. The stories which we tell in casual conversation may indeed be boring; they ramble on without any connecting middle and they may have no end. In biblical stories what comes in between may, indeed, need to be traced back to original, and sometimes disparate, sources which will have their own bearing on the story. But the originals cannot be allowed to dominate the direction of the storytelling. The final editor did see the incidents as a unified story. He may have done his editorial work poorly and we may conclude that he has told the story badly. But we must at least give him the initial presumption that he knew what he was doing before we begin to dissect the piece into its sources. One should be aware of a tendency among some scholars to over-stress an explanation of the sources to the disadvantage of the received text.

THE PLOT

Some stories center basically on plot. The point of the story is conveyed by relating certain actions which develop and carry along interest as we try to anticipate what will happen next. Such, for example, is the murder mystery. The fun of reading the story is in trying to outguess the problem-solver. The course of events contains various clues which are cleverly hidden and which either lead to the murderer or deliberately lead us astray. We are disappointed if at the end we find that the murder was committed haphazardly by a common thief who walked in off the street. So also we feel let down if some essential clue has been omitted. The story must hang together as a whole and each part must have a clear function. Science fiction in its simplest form is a plot story. A movie of such a story will need much action and immense amounts of scenery, top quality actors are not absolutely essential.

The story of the Passion of Jesus Christ is used here as an example
of a plot story. The story was the first continuous narrative to be put
together and although it is told differently by each of the four Gospels
it is still surprisingly consistent despite the variant details. The basic
events are:

1. The scene in the Garden of Olives leading up to the arrest of Jesus
2. The appearance of Jesus before the Sanhedrin
3. The referral of Jesus to Pilate and the deliverance to crucifixion
4. The incidents on the way to Golgatha
5. The cry of Jesus on the cross before he delivers up his spirit
6. The deliverance of the body for burial

In essence this is the story of the hero who failed. The events are
arranged to indicate that the victim was innocent, but his innocence
could not change his death. Later additions would alter the basic
message, but as far as a story is concerned, this is where the plot runs.
Without each of these incidents there would be no story. Any closer
examination of individual incidents in this story will need to consider
this plot as directive.

Of course, the Passion Story is much more complex than this brief
analysis indicates. It is also too familiar a story to make such a diagnosis
of plot do more than call attention to the basic theme. But there are
numerous stories, particularly in the Old Testament, which can be
read profitably if we simply ask: Where is this story going? Who did
what? What is the climax? For example, to go back to the first story
of the seven days of creation, we may ask: What is this story all about?
The seven days are a storyteller's technique for getting dramatic climax
into the story. The essential could be compressed into a lack-luster
statement that God made all things by his word and saw that they
were good. Such a statement is bland and unappealing. Strung out in
majestic and ordered presentation, the effect is dramatic. When the
creation of man is reached, the story expands to tell that man is made
in the image of God, male and female, and that they are given dominion
over lesser things. Then on the seventh day God rested. As a story
this is the climax. There must be special meaning to that. After all

the whirlwind activity, the world went on with God merely watching and blessing the day and proclaiming its holiness.

At this point the professional scholar is prepared to offer substantial information. If not corralled, he may do so almost endlessly. But some facts are worth noting. First, there are several ancient stories from the same cultural area which parallel this one in a rough way. These are human endeavors to express the concept of beginnings in some artistic way. None of them need to be justified scientifically since they were not scientific papers, but stories, mostly cultic. None of them need to be given a carelessly applied moral meaning. Yet there is a logic about the point being made as in any good story. The scholar knows that the biblical story was written no earlier than the time of the Babylonian Captivity (circa 597–539 B.C.), and in a situation where all the orderliness of life seemed to have vanished for the Chosen People. Instead of concluding that the world was a crazy, mixed-up place without purpose or order, the author clearly intended to say that he believed that God still ruled the disorderly world even though he seemed to be resting.

THE CHARACTERS

The other broad type of narrative centers around the development of characters rather than the plot. Plot stories need very little disclosure of how people feel, the motives they have, the emotional conflicts they experience, or the way in which they change. In plot stories the logic of the events leads straight to the conclusion and about all the reader needs to do is to finish the story to find out what it was all about. In a story based on character development the reader must be constantly asking: What is going on inside the characters? The events may not have much weight in indicating where the story is going and the speeches may seem to branch off at odd angles to one another. The story moves along as the characters are forced to reveal their inner selves.

A good example of such storytelling is found in John 7:53–8:11, the Woman Caught in Adultery. It is a good example in that we can definitely say that it is a complete story in itself. The evidence of the most ancient manuscripts is that these verses were inserted after the Gospel was completed; even the language sounds more like Luke than John. Somebody told this story simply as a story—whether factual or not makes no difference here. It has a beginning and an end within itself.

The story is simple. The scribes and Pharisees brought to Jesus a woman caught in adultery. They asked him if he thought the death penalty decreed by the law should be imposed. Jesus bent down and started tracing with his finger on the ground. When they persisted, he simply said, "Let the man among you who has no sin be the first to cast a stone at her." Then he continued his doodling. They drifted away and Jesus asked the woman if there was no one to condemn her. When she said no, he simply told her, "Nor do I condemn you. You may go. But from now on, avoid this sin."

The actions in the plot will not carry the story. All that happens by way of motion is that the scribes and Pharisees bring a woman to Jesus, he doodles on the ground, they leave, and the woman is dismissed. One cannot make a story out of that. Nor do the speeches dovetail with one another to explain how the conclusion is reached. They ask him a simple legal question. He gives them no answer, but does something with his finger on the ground. If he wrote some words, the storyteller does not deem it important to tell us what he wrote. When they persisted, he simply told them, "Let the man who is without sin cast the first stone." That saying really goes nowhere, although it raised the ancient question that legal systems try to avoid: Can the judgment be separated from the judge? His next speech is directed to the simple fact that they had left. Obviously, he could see that they had left so the question is directed at some other point. His final statement is that he does not condemn her. He says nothing about forgiveness or guilt; but he does tell her not to do it again. On the logic of actions or dialogue the story doesn't make much sense. Yet throughout the ages readers have made a great deal of sense out of it and know something about the conclusion.

If we ask how we arrive at our conclusion, we can only say that we are reading between the lines. We already expect the scribes and

Pharisees to be the villains and attribute to them some sinister motive in asking the question. The final editor added a note to make sure we did not miss this: "They were posing this question to trap him, so that they could have something to accuse him of." We know what the doodling is all about; he is challenging them to reveal themselves further. In Jesus' first reply we are immediately aware that he is the wise man. When they drift off, we read defeat into their action. But it is really the woman who is the catalyst in the story. The tension between good and bad would not be resolved without her. Oddly, the only line she has in the story is, "No one, sir." Yet we instinctively read into it a whole change of character. The villains stay villains to the last; the wise man becomes wiser still; but the woman has changed. Her change challenges us to re-examine our views on judgment. The character development in the story has involved us.

Such a reading of the story may, of course, be highly deceptive. The danger of reading between the lines may be precisely that there is nothing, or something quite different, to read. The lay reader, however, is in no greater danger than the professional. A scholar, who shall remain anonymous, wrote an article in a prestigious journal claiming that the solution to the problem lay in the action of the unmentioned husband who had hired witnesses to accuse the woman falsely. Perhaps that is what really did happen, but that is not the way the author told the story, and if he left out that decisive clue then the story vanishes as a story. The one fact that is clear is that the story of the Adulterous Woman is a good story.

The story as I have read it, is a study in character development or a psychological drama. Such stories are exceedingly common in the Bible. They are not told to prove anything; they are told to illustrate. They deal with people in crisis, people who change inwardly. From the story of the Garden of Eden to the last wild vision of dragons and falling stars in the Book of Revelations the pattern is repeated. The Yahwist tradition in the Old Testament and the Johannine presentation in the New are exceedingly strong in this technique of storytelling. Yet it is not confined to these books; they are simply mentioned as extraordinary examples.

How will you read such stories? At this point it may be useful to make a brief résumé of what we have covered. In reading a biblical story, first ask: What is this story about? The climax should be given first consideration, and if that seems decisive, the various clues or incidents leading up to it should be considered as important indicators of what the conclusion is all about. A second step is to ask: Who are the characters in this story? What are their names? How would I picture them? What kind of people are they? If the characters are sharply drawn and stand out, then perhaps the story relies precisely on this disclosure of character, and the search for clues should be not in the events but in the psychological indicators of how the characters change.

At this point, something should be said in favor of the professionals. They are the ones who unearth the specific data on dates, social conditions, historical facts, specific forms in which people at the time did write, traditions of composition, editing, and editorializing. Much of this is included under the general terms of historical criticism, form criticism, and redaction criticism. It is, of course, essential for defining the state of the original text. So also are textual and linguistic studies which have helped very much to produce a more accurate text and translations. The general reader very much needs such scholarly work in order to understand what the story was originally like to the first readers.

But the point of objectivity should not be overdone. No reader is ever objective, neither the professional nor the lay reader. We all bring our own suppositions and our own world to the reading of the text. We meet our own needs first of all. Instead of striving for an impossible objectivity, we should struggle for understanding both of the text and of ourselves. To say where both are and what they imply—to read between the lines, so to speak—is our primary concern.

This is particularly important in such psychological dramas as have been described here. In a plot story we may easily admit that we have never been in this situation ourselves and may never be. If the story has some personal meaning for us, we probably arrive at it by some fanciful imagining or hero worship. In a character story, however, we are immediately involved, for these people reflect our own experiences. Our acceptance of the story depends mostly on what we know of human nature in general, and more specifically, of what we know of ourselves. The experience is constantly changing in our own personal lives, in the social conditions around us, in world and ward politics, in laws of supply and demand, food, freedom, and so on. The experience is dynamic, alive both in the Bible and in us. The common element between story and us is that we are seeking a person—ourselves as well as the persons in the story.

SYMBOLS

In a plot story we seek for clues. The clues must be precisely ordered since they are already the conclusion in hidden form. The same should be said of symbols. They are clues to the final meaning and need to be considered carefully as foreshadowings of what is intended in the story. Determining the meaning of symbols is often an instantaneous process for us; it is at other times most complex, especially when the symbols come from an age and culture which is foreign to us.

Lest these generalities confuse rather than clarify, let me give an example. The Gospel of John tells the story of the meeting of Jesus and a Samaritan woman at the well of Jacob (cf. John 4:4–42). The dialogue begins when Jesus says to her, "Give me a drink." Since Jesus was sitting near a public well, the request seems straightforward and self-contained. Yet in his next speech (which ignores what the woman said), he puts a different meaning on "drink." "If only you recognized God's gift, and who it is that is asking you for a drink, you would have asked him instead, and he would have given you living water." It is clear that he is talking about something of which water is only a symbol. He is also talking about asking and seeking. Without relating the rest of the story, it is evident that this is what the conclusion is all about. Toward the end of the dialogue he remarks that the Father is seeking those who worship in spirit and truth. At that point the woman asks in her own way, "I know there is a Messiah coming. When he comes, he will tell us everything." He simply says, "I who speak to you am he." The seeking for water has found a total conclusion in the revelation of his person.

Without an understanding that the original request was purposely put in terms of seeking a drink of water, the discourse could not have reached its conclusion. If the exchanges between the woman and Jesus are analyzed, they will not be found to have much logical connection. The coquettish sallies of the woman are always countered with wise sayings that go off in a completely different direction. Slowly the pretended self-images and public images of this woman are stripped away. She is the town vamp, the daring one who flaunts convention in her forwardness and her men; she is then the religious bigot who can only quote ancient one-liners about a dispute which she does not understand. But finally she is revealed as a woman of simple faith who was afraid to disclose herself to the others. The story, much like the story of the Adulterous Woman, is a character development. But here the revelatory clue is found in the symbol of water.

Now this is relatively simple, especially if one is acquainted with the Gospel of John. Symbols play a great part in that Gospel; water is one of the more frequently used. Water symbolizes life; that is rather natural, but in John it always has a connotation of what he calls "eternal life." "Eternal" is present as well as future so the present reality mingles with the prophetic future.

Within the biblical translation, the symbols take on a permanence and life of their own from part to part. They have a history with a beginning and a multiple presence in biblical texts. Nor are they killed off by the closing of the Book. They persist in our own culture and many of them have meaning in our lives even when we are no longer familiar with the actuality. "The Lord is my shepherd" reverberates down through the ages. We know what the prophet Micaiah is talking about when he saw Israel scattered on the mountains like sheep without a shepherd (1 Kings 22:17); we get the impact of Ezechiel's vision of the rams butting the goats (Ezekiel 34:21); we are with Christ when he pictures himself as the Good Shepherd. We know what the meaning is although we may never have seen a live sheep and certainly do not have job experience as a shepherd. We do realize however, that whenever the word sheep is used in the Bible, it probably has a symbolic meaning and is saying something about us.

The problem being discussed here is simply the function of symbols within a story. The actual meaning and internal functioning of symbols is another and larger problem. For our purposes, however, we need only advert to the fact that symbols establish points of reference in a story and demand some sort of fulfillment if the story is to be well told. Otherwise, there is no reason for using the symbol in the story. In the example given, water was a symbol that got shaped in various ways. It already had a symbolic meaning from the Johannine use and from many previous uses in the Bible. The story shaped itself around a well and a woman who came to get water. Without that physical fact the story has no locale and no meaning. It ties the whole story together.

TRAGEDY, EPIC, AND COMEDY

Of the basic forms of stories, three are of special concern to me. The tragedy is most easy to define, perhaps because our literature has had such superb examples. Aristotle defined a tragedy as a tale about a hero who is destroyed by one fatal flaw, perhaps even a virtue. The tragedy is a self-contained story; it needs no introduction to fill us in on previous action and it concludes so absolutely that nothing more can be added. No one has ever written "Son of Hamlet" or "Macbeth II." Tragedy involves rigid logic; the tale sets up its own conditions of plot and character, and so leads by compulsion to the destruction of its hero. There can be no escape, no happy ending.

The Bible knows many tragedies. The first king of Israel, Saul, is a tragic figure (cf. 1 Samuel 8 to 2 Samuel 1). He is the hero who stands head and shoulders above the crowd in physical size, who is decisive with a large mind to organize a whole new political system. He is anointed by the priest-prophet Samuel and so has divine backing. His flaw is his own decisiveness; he never really surrenders to the God who made him king. At the end, Saul is half-demented and commits the supreme crime which he himself had outlawed. He goes to consult a witch who summons up the dead prophet Samuel. The old man is as implacable in death as in life; the sentence has been pronounced and nothing can avert the doom. So Saul is slain the next day. Fittingly, the story ends with a poignant poetic lamentation by David (2 Samuel 1).

Judas, of course, is the tragic figure of the New Testament. He was called "man of Karioth," the only apostle called by a place name—presumably a matter of some importance. None of the Gospels dispute his calling or his initial sincerity; it is the devil who first puts the thought of betrayal into his heart. The deed must be done and nothing can prevent it, as Jesus himself says. The last saying about Judas in all the Gospels is that he betrayed the Lord. The Acts of the Apostles describes his end more vividly, but it is not so much a question of blame as of the inevitability of a prophecy. It is the inescapable necessity which makes the story of Judas a tragedy, not his guilt.

The epic or saga (hero stories in poetry tend to be called epics and those in prose tend to be called sagas) is in some ways the obverse of the tragedy. The hero inevitably wins. The suspense comes from the perils to which the hero is exposed. But the reader knows from the start that the hero shall come out all right. Television viewers are completely familiar with this type of story; they know beforehand that within a half-hour or an hour, the detective will have solved the crime, the villain will be caught, or the doctor will have cured the patient. There are hero stories in the Bible, but fewer than you might expect. Esther, in its original telling, is a hero story; the stories of the heroes of the persecution in Maccabean times, as told in the Second Book of Maccabees, are hero stories although the heroes and heroines die and the genre is more often called "pathetic history." They do not die before they have vindicated themselves and their nation. Apocalyptic under its odd cloak of wild symbols is basically a hero story. The story of the chaste Susanna which was appended to the apocalyptic book of Daniel has nothing to do with apocalyptic, but it fits the tenor of the book because it is a hero story. Daniel routs his opponents in a way more satisfying than Perry Mason in a courtroom scene.

Some things should be noted about hero stories in whatever literature they occur. They are popular stories and their appeal lies largely in the fact that readers identify with the hero so readily. We all like to share the total victory of the hero and wish that we could be like that. Second, it is easy to move from the hero to the exemplar—the "go and do in like manner" story. Finally, the fact that the outcome is right seems to validate that the hero is right. Simply as a story, this is not at all required. There is a popular type of story called the spy thriller. The good spy wins, but he usually leaves behind a trail of deceit, infidelity, and slaughter. Leo Durocher's saying that "nice guys don't win" can be equally true in hero stories as in baseball.

These general remarks about hero stories cause endless difficulties in interpreting biblical stories. Actually, the Bible has no hero except God. Other victors are simply reflections of him and are usually fairly distorted reflections at that. Very few stories are told to give example of upright conduct. The Bible seems to follow the saying of the Psalmist: "There is not one who does good, not even one." Apparent victories abound but on closer examination prove to have a twist that reveals the hollowness of the victory. Abraham is a true hero of faith, but Joseph in Egypt is not. The stories of the early David are of the heroic Jesse James variety, but the story of King David is a much more sophisticated comedy. Hero stories are told which have the simple point of making the main character a hero, not an exemplar. Such are the hero stories told of Elisha and the wonders that he wrought, some of them apparently pointless or frivolous. The unjust judge of Christ's parable appears to be a hero even to God, but remains an unjust judge to the end. The New Testament knows very few heroes. Certainly Peter is not a hero nor are any of the other apostles. Christ himself is not a hero; he is either a tragic or a comic character depending on how much of the story one reads. By "comic" I do not mean ludicrous; I use the word with immense respect.

Comedy is, indeed, the most difficult form of storytelling. The comic or humorous emerges by placing disparate things together. Incongruity is at its heart. Yet the incongruity must be made to appear reasonable. An old vaudeville joke has it:

"Had some bad luck today. Ran over a milk bottle and cut my tire to pieces."
"Didn't you see it?"
"Nope. Kid had it hidden under his coat."

Jack Benny had a marvelous routine in which he was held up by a robber who said the traditional, "Your money or your life." Benny would pause interminably until the hold-up man prodded him again, and then Benny would say, "Alright, alright; I'm thinking about it." The style and technique in comedy is all important. A pink elephant is incongruous, but merely cute on a baby's crib. A pink elephant running in the Kentucky Derby would be hilarious, but one would need to devise a plot in which it became inevitable that this pink elephant was a real contender.

It is said that there are only five good jokes in the world. Whatever they are, the examples given always deal with serious things such as life and death, heaven and hell, God and us, sex, and nature. Good jokes, like good comedy, come to grips with essential problems. The logic which we know is turned upside down to reveal something of a world in which our logic would not prevail. This is comedy at its best, a spoofing of reason while using reason.

In this sense the Bible has many comic stories. Jonah is a deliberately funny story. It mocks all the narrowminded ideas that God must act as we think he should. This prophet (whose name is taken from the one prophet of success in the Old Testament—cf. 2 Kings 14:25) tries in a most unprophetlike way to escape the Lord since his mission is to the hated Gentiles. When he finally preaches to the evil inhabitants of Nineveh, they immediately repent in magnificent fashion. When Jonah complains that the Lord is softhearted, the Lord consoles Jonah by growing a bush overnight to protect him from the sun while he waits for the catastrophe to hit Nineveh. Then he sends a worm to eat the plant. The final line is best of all: "Should I not be concerned over Nineveh, the great city, in which there are more than a hundred and twenty thousand persons who cannot distinguish their right hand from their left, not to mention the many cattle?" It was a stroke of genius to mention those cattle who were also doing penance in sackcloth.

The Book of Judges concludes with two dissociated short stories. One of them tells the bloodthirsty story of the civil war against Benjamin during which all the young women of Benjamin are slaughtered. All the Israelites have sworn that they will not allow their daughters to marry any surviving Benjaminites. As they then realize, they have virtually condemned one tribe in Israel to extinction. Yet there must be twelve tribes; such is the tradition which expresses the will of God. They are trapped in a necessity which they themselves have devised. So they arrange that at the next religious gathering at Shiloh the Benjaminite men will be allowed to stage a mock raid and carry off some of the women. As Robert Boling has remarked, the Rape of the Shiloh Virgins is a truly comic story.

And so it goes. The long story of Joseph in Egypt in Genesis, chapters 37 to 50, seems at first reading to be a hero story—Hebrew boy makes good and becomes Prime Minister of Egypt. At the end, however, is the comic element that Joseph, who manipulated his brothers so adroitly and cruelly, suddenly realizes that he himself has been used by God. The so-called Succession Narrative (1 Kings 7 to 2 Kings 2) which tells of how Solomon, a most unlikely candidate, became the successor to King David is a comic story in which David does everything wrong only to have the conclusion come out right.

In the New Testament Luke's story of the Infancy has its comic note. The hero is introduced as one "called the Son of the Most High." The God who dwells in light inaccessible sends his son into the world as a baby. That he is conceived by a virgin is entirely fitting and in some ways inevitable. Tales of a virgin mother had long satisfied a human need to explain how the god got into human form. The story ends with the appointment of a new servant of God, but nobody, including the boy's mother, understands this.

The basic story of Jesus is, of course, the most comic of all. He is a tragic hero, inevitably consigned to death. He is too honest and his virtue finally destroys him. Politics, human pettiness, and supermundane evil enters in, but it is basically his own will which propels him to destruction. And when the tragedy has run its course, he is raised from the dead and begins a new and victorious life which once more appears to be more tragic than triumphal.

To speak of stories of Jesus as comic is in no way to impugn their dignity or their seriousness or their factuality—even *we* say that fact is stranger than fiction. The only point being made is that if a story is to be told at all, it must be told in a certain way. Even God does not escape that. Comedy is one way of telling a story and a most sophisticated one. Comedy is not a flight from reason. The true comedy has its own logic and inevitability, but it is not the conventional wisdom. It escapes into that realm where we come to grips with unexplainable facts which point to a world beyond our ordered way of thinking. If the stories of the Bible are not read with this possibility in mind, they may become tyrannical outbursts of imperatives rather than creative stories which lead us to a higher realm.

TENSION AND CLIMAX

A fairy tale usually ends "And they lived happily ever after." The tale must end there because not much of a story can be made of people who live happily ever after. A dragon or a bear or a witch or something must be in the story to create tension. It is so with more realistic stories. There must always be the "good guys" and the "bad guys." Without conflicting forces there is no story.

Biblical stories cannot work without paying attention to the conflicting forces. The question, for example, is not whether there is a theological proof for the Devil, but whether any story can work as a story without a touch of the Devil. The evil forces may be portrayed as human enemies—the "nations," the "scribes and Pharisees," those "whose god is their belly," "they picked up stones to stone him," "Herod sought to kill the child," "Crucify him!" But there is also an awareness in the Bible that evil is more pervasive and tenacious than ordinary human opposition. The evil is cosmic. In the Old Testament "chaos" appears in many forms—in the unruly waters, in sea monsters, in darkness and the abyss; in the New Testament it turns up as Belial, the Evil One, "the power of darkness," "those who sin against the Holy Spirit," and eventually as dragons, the man on the black horse, and so on. Finally, the evil forces often appear subtly within the person who is the hero. Saul has an evil spirit which drives him to destruction; the Pharisees are "beside themselves"; even Christ is accused of having a demon, a *daimon*, a force which drives him on uncontrollably. Nicodemus can never make up his mind and remains a taunting figure about whom we say "Did he or didn't he?" Something inexplicable is wrong with Nicodemus. The world is not a simple and friendly place in biblical lore; it is filled with dark caves of violence and doubt. You can decide personally whether these are realities; you cannot ignore them if the stories are to make sense as stories.

The element of conflict in biblical stories is exceedingly high. The Bible does not toy with petty human abnormalities; there are no stories in the Bible about people who are simply feeling bad as we all do and need sympathy; nor are we simply presented with the more serious problems of wayward children or psychopaths. There is a devil involved; the evil is clear-eyed and willful. Israel is responsible for rejecting its God; Jerusalem is a whore; the nations are the seat of demons; Jesus is murdered by powers on high which are far more powerful than a mere Pilate or "the Jews." The stories are often not for the queasy; blood runs, Jezabel is eaten by dogs, bears devour the boys who jeer at Elisha, the Jews in the story of Esther slaughter their enemies mercilessly, Jesus tells a would-be disciple to leave the dead to bury the dead, the Jews will not leave Jesus alone even in death but post a guard over the body, and the Book of Revelation drips with the blood of martyrs and foes.

To all this conflict there must be a climax, but finding it is not always easy. Tragedy has the clearest climax. In such a story the ending is totally sufficient; there is no possibility of redemption or of another chance. The hero story, on the other hand, invites repetition. We are never satisfied with one marvelous victory, whether of God or of man. The Hebrew storytellers spoke endlessly of the wondrous deeds of Yahweh. The noncanonical Gospels and Acts of Apostles in New Testament times created more hero stories of a more and more fanciful kind about Jesus, Peter, and especially Paul. The hero story is open-ended, always urging new adventures. And yet we ask "Is there some end somewhere to the basic hero story?"

Scholars are much concerned about the eschatological element in the Bible, the "end time" or the climax. The biblical literature as a whole is more concerned with the present than with the past even when it tells stories about the past. Yet to the biblical writers history was something more than an endless cycle. The stories of the various peoples were going somewhere. However, the final outcome was wrapped in mystery. To express such ideas the apocalyptic form of writing was developed. Basically, apocalyptic is a hero story. The conflict arises on a more than human level. The war is between dragons and angels, stars and moons falling from the heavens, mighty armies that clash by night. If a theologian had written an abstract treatise about this, he would have concluded that since God is almighty there could not be the slightest defeat on his part. But the apocalyptist was more realistic despite his wild symbol language. Even with an almighty God, the outcome of the battle always appears in doubt to the foot soldiers. It was then an act of faith to make the story come out with a clear-cut victory. The various vignettes in apocalyptic must always be interpreted with this in mind. The conquering forces of evil never remain triumphant; the conquering forces of good never sweep the field completely. As a story it is always dynamic; it never reaches a point of quiet and equilibrium. Something more is always to be added.

Comedy reaches a climax with the raising of a question about how much we really understand. To solve the problem of comedy is to destroy the story. It is like explaining a joke. I have referred to the story of the Rape of the Shiloh Virgins as an example of comedy. To devise elaborate explanations of how the matter can be legally justified by various Hebraic laws or social customs is to destroy the story. The climax is found precisely in the inevitability of two logical actions coming in conflict with one another and posing for us the problem of how we shall view the solution.

HISTORICAL NARRATIVE

Reading the Bible as history is, perhaps, the most delicate exercise of all. "History" seems to mean factual description to us. That is not really the whole truth about history as a form of writing, but the conviction has a strong hold on us. Our culture has further exaggerated the impression as far as the Bible is concerned; we say "That is Gospel truth." Additionally, I presume that most of my readers already have a faith commitment toward the historicity of the Bible, even if it is the faith in the denial of some or all of the events. In fact, the personal equation is so important in this matter that it would be well before reading the Bible as history to set out one's own personal expectations of the historical accuracy of the Bible. My purpose here is not to advocate faith conclusions, but simply to examine what the general concept of historical writing is all about and how it appears in the Bible.

The dictionary definitions of history all begin by saying that history deals with past events. That is our understanding of the word, but it does not tell us *how* history deals with past events. Property deeds at the local courthouse are a way of recording past events and an exceedingly important one for all social history. But they are not history. Making a tape recording of an event is not really "recording history"; playing it back may be an invitation to boredom and confusion. Not all events are important. The editor of the Gospel of John noted that, "There are still many other things that Jesus did, yet if they were written about in detail, I doubt that there would be room enough in the entire world to hold the books to record them." (John 21:25) It is an exaggeration, of course, but a legitimate one. Historical writing implies that a selection has already been made.

To follow the writer of history we must understand how he or she intended the events to function in the selection which was made. Simple records may be included in a history, but they are not the heart of the matter. The Bible is familiar with the difference between record and history and rejects record in most instances. In the Book of Kings the stories about the individual kings always end with a formula: "The rest of the acts of So-and-So with all that he did are recorded in the book of the Chronicles of the kings of Judah/Israel." Are the chronicles of the kings of Judah and Israel history? They did exist as some sort of official court record and presumably they were factual. However, the writers of the Books of Kings were not interested in this kind of record. They were not even interested in them as footnotes which would prove the veracity of their own descriptions. They simply set them aside as something unimportant for their purposes. The events they did relate functioned in quite a different fashion. If we are to follow their historical writing, we must know something about how they intended the events to function in their overall plan.

We tend to assume that the function of history is to validate the facts. That is more of a procedure for a court of law than for an historian. The function of good history is to enlighten us to understand human events. We presume that the events did happen, but we are willing to concede a more-or-less in this matter and to look for larger issues and even for different ways of approaching the enlightenment. So, for example, we may read a history of the First World War and say, "That's a good book. There are a few facts that I doubt and some of the opinions that I can't agree with, but it is a well-told history." Or we may read an historical novel about the same period and say, "That's fiction, but it is a lot more real than most histories." The kind of truth which we are trying to get at is not simply factual. So it is not accidental that the words "history" and "story" look very much alike in our English vocabulary. The reality of the truth we are looking for also looks very much like both story and history, but there is a difference.

On the question of factuality, the auxiliary sciences can give but little direct help to understand the story element. Archaeologists have discovered that King Omri of Israel (reigned 876–869 B.C.; cf. 1 Kings 16:21–28) is also recorded on the Mesha Stone as the conqueror of Moab and in the Assyrian chronicles as the founder of the House of Omri. The name undoubtedly refers to the biblical character, but tells us nothing beyond that about the factuality of the biblical story of Omri. The biblical story does not even mention his campaign against Moab. Numerous such bits of information have been verified from archaeology, epigraphy, and linguistic studies. 2 Kings 20:20 refers to the "pool and conduit by which water was brought into the city" during the reign of King Hezekiah. The conduit is well known and an inscription has been found in the center of the tunnel telling of how it was built during Hezekiah's time. But this tells us nothing at all about the character and story of Hezekiah as the Bible describes him. According to some scholars recent finds in Syria, at Ebla, seem to indicate that the divine name "Ya" (as in Yahweh) was used long before the time of Abraham, but this does not tell us much about the story of how God chose Abraham. Taken together, such facts reveal a good deal about the social or political or religious situations described in the Bible, particularly in the Old Testament. It is not possible to regard the history of the Bible as simply a made-up story. But direct verification of the stories that are told is impossible because no other records exist that tell the same stories in the same way or refute them.

The science of biblical criticism is helpful in other ways, particularly in defining the forms and functions of types of writing. Such analysis depends largely on having multiple samples of similar materials to compare. Matthew, Mark, and Luke, for example, are similar accounts. It is their commonality which allows us to analyze set forms of writing within them and then to understand something of the different functions of each Gospel as we see this material used in different ways. So also the Books of Kings and the Books of Chronicles both treat the stories of the kings of Judah, and much of the material is the same. Sometimes we have similar materials presented in different literary forms. Exodus 1 to 2 Samuel tells the story of the Chosen People from the deliverance from Egypt to the reign of King David. The same story is told in Psalm 78. The prose story functions as some sort of community remembrance of the past for understanding the present; the poetry of Psalm 78 functions as a liturgy of praise to God in the Temple.

The analysis of forms enables us to understand something of the functions. Neither Psalm 78 nor the story of early Israel functioned as historical proof. Nor were any of the Gospels written to prove facts to the pagans; the form indicates that they were written to second generation Christians to exhort them to live up to the insights which the authors had of the Christ event. In fact, most of the Biblical accounts which we are accustomed to think of as historical were intended more for personal and community mediation and self-examination than for proof.

The uniqueness of this historical approach emerges if we compare the Bible to other ancient records. The Gospel format was a unique literary form, probably created by Mark, to express religious insights about the story he was telling. There is nothing like it in other ancient literature. So also in the Old Testament the manner of relating royal story is unique. For example, we have isolated a form of coronation story called a *Königsnovellen*. The set form called for a vision which the king had before his inauguration; in the vision he was granted certain gifts by the god; then he built a temple to commemorate the event.

Obviously, this functioned as a divine affirmation for the authority of the king or Pharaoh.

The story of Solomon begins with an ancient story of a dream which he had at Gibeon, goes on to tell of how he asked God for the gift of wisdom, and this serves as an introduction to the long account of how he built the Temple. The format seems to parallel the pagan literary type, but the function and use of the material is quite different. The biblical material seems to be drawn from historical recollections of some sort; the total story of Solomon seems to be shaped around the inaugural vision and the conclusion of the whole story is that Solomon was a most foolish king. A pagan author would have been horrified at using a *Königsnovellen* in this way; the biblical author was creatively unique. He might shape the material more or less to conform to standard procedures and in doing so might "romanticize" his materials, but he had his own purposes in doing so. In this book and among mainline scholars, frequent use is made of the expression "historical nucleus." As historians we sometimes do not know precisely how historical a story is, although there is often ample evidence that there is something factual behind it. How much historical fact we need for faith assertions is a theological question.

AN EXAMPLE—THE BOOK OF RUTH

The Book of Ruth is chosen as an example since the beginning and ending of the story is clearly marked out by the text itself as a separate and complete story. The origin of the story is usually traced to the tenth century B.C., but if an alternate opinion of dating it to the 5th century B.C. is adopted, the analysis of the story as such will not really be different. The literary form is consistent and as pure as anything in the Old Testament; divergent sources or extensive re-editing are not really problems. Moreover, it is one of the highest artistic achievements of the storyteller's art. In this case, the earliest is among the best.

The cast of characters is simple:

Naomi—a Hebrew wife and mother who went with her husband and two sons as a pioneer to the plains of Moab. In a pagan land her faithfulness and self-reliant strength held the family together amid disasters. Her name means "the amiable or pleasant one."

Ruth—the Moabite girl who married one of Naomi's sons. She is beautiful, unswerving in her loyalty to Yahweh and Naomi, and submissive to her mother-in-law. She returns to Bethlehem with Naomi.

Boaz—a rich landowner of Bethlehem, a regal character who helps the impoverished women and at the end marries Ruth.

God—God is here called Yahweh, the distinctively Hebraic name. He never appears directly in the action, but is quite clearly pictured as operating behind the scenes throughout.

There are minor characters, but they need not detain us.

The plot is also simple. In Act One which sets the stage, Naomi had gone uncomplainingly with her husband and two sons to Moab to escape a famine in Judah. Disaster soon struck and the husband died. Nonetheless, Naomi made a living somehow for the next ten years and saw her sons married to admirable Moabite girls. Then disaster struck a second time and the two sons died, childless. Naomi decided to return alone to Bethlehem. One of the girls, Ruth, refused to leave either Naomi or Yahweh. So the two women set out for Bethlehem. When they arrived, the women at the village well greeted Naomi with astonishment. "Can this be Naomi?" they asked. Indeed, the "pleasant one" was a different kind of woman. "I went away with an abundance, but the Lord has brought me back destitute," she said bitterly.

Act Two is set in Bethlehem at the time of the barley harvest. The ancient custom said that the harvesters should leave some of the grain for the poor to glean. Naomi sent Ruth out into the fields. It happened that she went to the field of Boaz. He was much taken by this beautiful girl, inquired about her, urged her to stay in his fields, instructed his workmen to help her, and even invited her to eat with him. When Ruth reported all of this to Naomi, the widow immediately recognized a good thing. She knew of Boaz, a near kinsman, and a rich one at that. So she instructed Ruth to continue with him. As the barley harvest neared its end, Naomi realized that the time had come for decisive action. Flaunting all custom, she had Ruth dress in what finery she could manage, go out in the evening and sleep beside Boaz at the threshing floor. In the morning Boaz discreetly had her leave early and sent her home with abundant food. All that Naomi said was, "Wait here, my daughter, until you learn what happens, for the man will not rest, but will settle the matter today."

Act Three is set at the city gates. The storyteller has not told us how the men of the village happened to gather for a formal, legal meeting. All we are told is that Naomi had put up for sale a piece of property which she still owned. There was a catch to the purchase; in accordance with the ancient custom the man who bought the property would also need to marry Ruth and have children by her. The closest of kin had the first bid, but backed off when he learned that he would also need to marry Ruth since he did not want to dilute his children's inheritance. So Boaz stepped forward, and in a curious legal act of handing over sandals, closed the deal.

Act Four tells of how Boaz and Ruth were married and in due time a son was born to them. Now a curious thing happens in the story. Boaz and Ruth, the happy couple, fade from the scene. The village women come to Naomi and sing the birth song. " 'Blessed is the LORD who has not failed to provide you today with an heir! May he become famous in Israel! He will be your comfort and the support of your old age, for his mother is the daughter-in-law who loves you. She is worth more to you than seven sons!' Naomi took the child, placed him on her lap, and became his nurse."

Such is the plot. At the climax of the story there is simply Naomi sitting there, holding the child. What is she thinking? Is this the pleasant Naomi or the bitter Naomi? Is she the victor or the victim of her manipulations? Who won? Should we admire or pity Naomi? With exquisite artistry the storyteller answers none of these questions. That is for you to think about.

What kind of story do we have here? If it is made to revolve around Boaz and Ruth, then we have a hero story. These are two good people, faithful to God, and representative of a generous, hospitable way of living. They fall in love, marry, and are rewarded with a child who will be great in Israel. They become exemplars of pious living.

However, they are rather static characters. Ruth is almost too good to be true; she is attractive, obedient, loving, and nothing can change that. Boaz is somewhat larger than life, a rich man who is magnanimous in all his dealings. Their story is edifying, but a bit too cut and dried to have a realistic cutting edge.

Naomi is really the catalyst in the story. She changes. First it is her virtue which leads her to be an exemplary Hebrew wife and then her bitterness which provides the conflict element. She, too, had had her love story both with Yahweh and with her husband. But her husband had been taken away from her and she fingered her other lover as the villain. In a way Naomi is a female Job. When her God failed, she took events into her own hands. The storyteller clearly pictures Naomi as a take-charge woman who manipulated both Boaz and Ruth. And when her victory was won, she might well have felt vindicated. But this is not the point the storyteller wants to reach. In the scene at the well he has Naomi say, "Do not call me Naomi. Call me Mara, for the Almighty has made it very bitter for me. I went away with an abundance, but the Lord has brought me back destitute. Why should you call me Naomi, since the Lord has pronounced against me and the Almighty has brought evil upon me?" At the end, the storyteller has the village women singing, "Blessed is the LORD who has not failed to provide you today with an heir!" The two speeches interlock. Naomi had changed once; did she change again? Who knows? The story is basically a comedy in which the God behind the scenes has apparently worked his own designs.

Either the original storyteller or a later editor added a geneology that highlighted a fact the readers already knew. The child of Boaz and Ruth was Obed and Obed was the grandfather of King David. There is a foreshadowing of future developments in this. The story is not part of the "official" Deuteronomist history which runs from Joshua to 2 Kings. It was a separate, almost private, story from the beginning, told mostly for its own enjoyment. Yet it also had something to add to that theme of election. The election was strange indeed. The great-grandmother of Israel's most successful man was a pagan girl. Matthew in his geneology of Jesus remembers it. The pagan girl was a symbol that the chosen people was larger than the Israelites.

PRACTICAL SUGGESTIONS

A few practical suggestions may be summarized from the pre-
ceding material. The nub of the question is intention, your intention
and the writer's intention. What is it in the reading of the story that
you are seeking? Proof? Example? Doctrinal statements? Enjoyment?
Thought-provoking problems? We all have such unclarified expectations and it is no easy task to bring them to the surface as we read.

The second essential is to define the intention of the author. This
is a complex task which can be approached only indirectly. Our sole
tool is the literary form which the ancient writers used. The auxiliary
sciences of archaeology, linguistics, comparative religion, and so forth,
can be of limited value. These are areas for experts and you will need
a good basic commentary.

Finally, we come to what we can do by reading the stories as we
would read other stories. It is surprisingly helpful simply to list the
characters in the story and to try to describe what kind of persons we
feel them to be. We can then look at the plot and ask whether it
develops by the actions or the character changes of the people involved.
Most likely we shall find a mixture. The climax of the story must be
pinpointed; if the story is a good one, the climax is already anticipated
in the clues or symbols. Most stories fall into the categories of tragedy,
hero stories, or comedy. Knowing this, we can make some suppositions
about what the author was trying to say as his basic theme. However,
we may need help here. The Bible is one book and the themes tend
to carry over from one area into another. The connection is not always
developmental or logical; there are gaps, new beginnings, and re-
interpretations of previous motifs. This part of the study is usually
called "biblical theology" or the history of the traditions. Since it is
broader than any one story which we shall read, we shall need some help
to identify the themes which are frequently carried on by symbols.

Despite the continuity of certain themes and symbols in the Bible,
we are unable to unify them all and say, "there is the heart of the
matter." Father Abraham is a symbol of faith and much swings around
that idea. But not all. Covenant and Promise have been proposed as

central axes of the Old Testament. It works, but only to a degree. Love, of course, has been stated with much certainty as the one essential teaching of the Bible. It is undoubtedly true—to a certain extent. Knowledge, freedom, power, mystery, and many other ideas have been set forth as central themes. Salvation history was a dominant perspective in Roman Catholic circles for a while after Vatican Council II. All have something to commend them; all eventually are pushed too far and too simplistically and we must at last escape their oppressive force. Perhaps the only true common denominator is that the Bible concerns persons, including God as a person or persons. We may as well admit that we are never going to unlock completely the complexities of all these persons, either human or divine.

For ourselves, the final fruit of reading the Bible need only be that we become better persons. We can be helped by other persons whether they come to us personally to join in discussion or whether we find them in books. But if we are true to the Bible itself we shall admit the need for another kind of person. Many a family Bible has a prayer at the beginning asking for enlightenment by the Holy Spirit. One may have a very personal understanding of what this means, but the need is obvious.

FOUR

Reading the Laws

SORTING OUT THE "LEGAL" SAYINGS

Calling this chapter "Reading the Laws" will cause difficulty, but it is best to face the unavoidable head-on. The laws embrace a vast diversity of reflections on human conduct and great sensitivity is needed to understand what is intended. We say, "Don't make a decision on rumor." We also say, "File your income tax return before April 15th." Both are expressed by an imperative verb, but they are not equally imperative. You may take or leave the first one; if you ignore the second, the government will get you. Yet we associate both with some sort of law. The Bible says, "Be perfect as your heavenly Father is perfect" (Matthew 5:48)—which is clearly impossible; it also says, "Do not kill" (Exodus 20:13)—which is obviously necessary but which neither the Bible nor any church can enforce; and it says, "Cast out the incestuous man" (1 Corinthians 5:13)—which Paul intended the Corinthians to do. Laws, precepts, exhortations, advice, and simple reflection are mixed up in the Bible. If every statement in the imperative is interpreted in the same way, we shall be in great trouble without ever realizing that the difficulty springs from the lack of focus in our use of the adjective "legal" or the noun "law."

LAW CODES AND LAW ENFORCEMENT

Civil law is enacted by a government for the protection and well-being of its citizens. It is obeyed by them and policed by the authorities. Individual laws are interpreted and due penalties meted out by the courts. With more or less sophistication, every society uses such a system of laws and enforcement and it works out more or less. We have our own sayings which reflect on the more or less. We say, "It is better not to make laws than to make them and not enforce them": or "The fewer the laws and the briefer, the better." Our experience of law seems to indicate that there is something behind law which can never be completely controlled. The ancients said: the gods made the laws; more often than not, we simply shrug our shoulders and try again.

In the course of time the laws develop into a body of law. We speak of codes of law. Sometimes the code is organized logically around principles and appropriate titles for application, as in the Code Napoleon or in the Code of Canon Law within the Roman Catholic Church. In our English legal tradition the code of law develops more or less haphazardly as collections of legislative bills are accumulated and as the courts interpret them and so produce precedents. The laws are sometimes codified by nothing more than being printed in one book. We still cling to the concept that all of this is a code and so speak of the Civil Code of the State of Illinois, for example. The function of this immense apparatus of legislators, judges, lawyers, police, and jailors is to ensure that people will perform or not perform acts for the benefit of the people.

We have a considerable body of laws from the ancient Near East. Most of them are preserved on some durable material such as clay or stone; that they were meant to endure is note-worthy. The best-known of them is that of Hammurabi who ruled from 1728 to 1686 B.C. in Mesopotamia. The prologue notes that, "I established law and justice in the language of the land, thereby promoting the welfare of the people"; the epilogue reveals a more pragmatic purpose for erecting the permanent basalt column on which the Code was inscribed, "In order that the strong might not oppress the weak, that justice might be dealt the orphan and the widows . . . . I wrote my precious words on my stela (the basalt stone), and in the presence of the statue of me, the king of justice, I set it up in order to administer the law of the land, to proscribe the ordinances of the land, to give justice to the oppressed. I am the king who is preeminent among kings; my words are choice, my ability has no equal." In between the prologue and the epilogue are some two hundred and eighty-two specific laws. Some of them are quite interesting. "If outlaws have congregated in the establishment of a woman wine-seller and she has not arrested those outlaws and did not take them to the palace, that wine-seller shall be put to death." "If a rowboat rammed a sailboat and has sunk it, the owner of the boat whose boat was sunk shall in the presence of the god set forth the particulars regarding whatever was lost in his boat and the one in charge of the rowboat which sank the sailboat shall make good to him his boat and his lost property." The laws of Hammurabi are generally reasonable although they tend to be very class conscious and are harsh in their punishments. However, the function of Hammurabi's Code as written on the basalt column should be noted: it was to protect the weak against the strong and to glorify the strongest among them all, namely Hammurabi.

We also speak of moral codes and moral laws. These are not enactments of governments, but dictates of conscience, however we may understand that such imperatives come about. No police force supervises them; no judge imposes sentences. People are inclined to interpret natural blessings or catastrophes as rewards or punishments attached to a moral code, but the cause and effect relationship is never very clear or unchallenged. Like civil codes, moral codes may be more or less systematized. On a professional level, we speak of a science of ethics although today's professionals are rather inclined to doubt that they have an entirely scientific discipline on their hands. Of such moral codes there are but fragmentary evidences in the ancient literature outside the Bible. Good living was connected with the will of the gods in some vague way; occasional wise men or storytellers grappled with the problem of good and evil, but never in a very disciplined way. Virtue was more a matter of good citizenship than of personal responsibility.

And this brings us to another way of speaking of codes, namely that of a lifestyle. Dress codes for companies or schools, family codes of conduct, the codes of the "in-group" or of society's elite or street gangs, and many other such codes exist without ever having been legislated. Their function is to identify us with a group. Breaking these laws generally leads to eviction from the group. "They" are no longer "one of us." Penalties are usually drastic although the code violation may be petty. The softening influence of religion may perhaps be seen in ceremonial codes which also function in a somewhat parallel way. There is a precise way of performing cultic actions, but the ceremonial code usually includes other rituals for righting the cultic faults in a benign manner.

All of this complicated description is intended simply to alert you to the many ways in which imperatives must be read in the Bible. If the Ten Commandments were a complete civil, moral, and cultic code which sets the one approved lifestyle and which was further detailed by various other sections of the Bible, we could read every passage in the same way and make sense of it. Even the most cursory approach to the Bible, however, recognizes that matters are not this easy. We make no bones about ignoring the Old Testament prescriptions for animal sacrifices; we take some of Paul's sayings about women's roles with a grain of salt; we have our own views on Christ's sayings about marriage and divorce, on resistance and nonresistance. We are perhaps not quite sure why we make such adjustments although the pick-and-choose method is obviously defective if there is nothing more to it than our personal likes and dislikes. It is necessary to take a look at some of the larger areas of such materials in order to ask: How should we read them? If they are intended to function as rules which some police agency would enforce, that is one thing; if they are simply advice or reflections on living, that is quite another. Many other shades of meaning lie in between. The final result will not be entirely satisfactory; even Paul had an ambivalent attitude toward law.

THE FUNCTION OF MORAL TEACHING

This much can be said with some sense of security; the principal emphasis in the Bible is on moral law, not civil. Some attempts have been made to picture the Mosaic Law as the constitutional law of the Monarchy, but the attempt has not been very successful. Whatever the operating civil law under the Monarchy was, it is not recorded as such in the Bible. In a somewhat similar way the Sermon on the Mount in Matthew 5 to 7 is sometimes called the New Law, but it really has little to say about any civil affairs or even about church government. In the rest of the New Testament the same lack of interest in civil law is manifest with only some few exceptions. Some broad statements are made about the relationship of apostles and churches to God and people; some specific advice is given about handling problems of dissent within the community; some few things are said about a proper attitude toward the civil government out there. But this is not the center of gravity.

In fact, the idea of a code as code is the most strikingly missing element in the biblical presentation. The Ten Commandments might be thought of as a code. All of the individual sayings in that collection are found in one way or another in other ancient laws and, insofar as societal duties are concerned, in most modern ones as well. The biblical list is a stroke of genius in brevity and order as compared to such a conglomeration as the two hundred and eighty-two case laws of the Code of Hammurabi. Yet the code does not seem to have had a great deal of impact. The Ten Commandments are listed only twice in the Bible in slightly variant forms in Exodus 20:1–17 and Deuteronomy 5:6–21; they are not cited completely in the New Testament at all.

More basic is the fact that it is our language which has termed them the ten "commandments." The original reference was to the ten "words," as in the Greek derivative "decalog." A "word" in biblical usage means a revelation, especially in such phrases as "the word of God." The word reveals something of who God is in relationship to us. In the final revelation, as phrased by the Gospel of John, it is Jesus Christ who is revealed as the Word of God. This application of revelation of a person as applying to law can be seen in the Sermon on the Mount in Matthew 5. The Sermon introduces the topic of the law very early: "Do not think that I have come to abolish the law and the prophets. I have come, not to abolish them, but to fulfill them." Then it goes on to talk about the kind of fulfillment which is meant. Two of the sayings in the Decalog are cited specifically: against murder and adultery. The other five examples are taken from other legislation on divorce, oaths, an eye for an eye, and a misuse of the injunction to love one's own countryman. The nub of the fulfillment is not in additional laws, but in a deeper understanding of our godlike potential for rising to heights of concern for others until we strive to become perfect as God is perfect. The function of the Sermon is not to establish more laws but to call the reader to a deeper wisdom.

This seems to have been the fundamental attitude of both the Old Testament Jew and the New Testament Christian in regard to the law. In the Old Testament, "law" was used to refer not simply to the Decalog and the annexed legislation, but to the whole body of story, poetry, and wise counsel which was the heritage of the people. The part of it contained in the first five books of the Old Testament was specifically referred to as the Torah. Torah has many meanings and nuances, but central to them all in actual function is the concept of instruction given and received. So the Psalmist caught the idea in his picture of the good life:

> (Happy the man who) meditates on his law day and night.
>
> Psalm 1:2

Psalm 119 has 176 verses, each of which mentions some aspect of the Law. Typical is Psalm 119:17–18:

> Be good to your servant, that I may live
>   and keep your words.
> Open my eyes, that I may consider
>   the wonders of your law.

The law was much more a source of meditation and of measuring the experience of living than it was a proof-text for right or wrong actions.

This is not to say that the laws did not have a legal function within that society. Paul pictures the Law as a tutor for the young (cf. Galatians 4:1–2), and that image is important for understanding law in the whole of the Bible. For example, Leviticus 17 to 26 is usually called the Code of Holiness. Much of it describes the ceremonials of

Temple worship, but intermingled are laws for society. The way in which these laws are presented is noteworthy; they center on the motivation behind the keeping of laws. Chapter 19 begins "The LORD said to Moses, 'Speak to the whole Israelite community and tell them: Be holy, for I, the LORD, your GOD, am holy.'" What follows is a list of various actions which the Israelite community can do to become holy as God is holy. The alternate formula is a simple, "I am the LORD." So we have, "You shall not bear hatred for your brother in your heart. Though you may have to reprove your fellow man, do not incur sin because of him. Take no revenge and cherish no grudge against your fellow countrymen. You shall love your neighbor as yourself. I am the LORD." (Leviticus 19:17–18) Civil rights legislation is represented in the saying, "When an alien resides with you in your land, do not molest him. You shall treat the alien who resides with you no differently than the natives born among you; have the same love for him as for yourself; for you too were once aliens in the land of Egypt. I, the LORD, am your GOD." (Leviticus 19:33–34) It is perfectly clear in such sayings that the function of the laws was not primarily to make community living better, but to offer to each person and to the community the potential of imitating the Lord God. So the final phrase of the fifth chapter of Matthew flows easily from the tradition, "Be perfect (or holy) as your heavenly Father is perfect." (Matthew 5:48)

If this was the primary function of Torah, then the laws must be read both on a primary level which conveys the spiritual message and on a secondary level which backs up societal rules. Murder, adultery, false oaths, stealing, taking care of the family, and so on, were taken quite seriously. Both in the Old Testament times when Israel lived under its own government and in times (much more frequent) when it lived under the government of others, and in New Testament times when there was no question of a Christian government, the Chosen People lived under civil legislation which was more or less common. Police and law courts and jails and executioners were part of the apparatus. The Bible did not establish such civil arrangements, though in general, it approved of them. It did confront them, however, and it gave a quite different interpretation to what lay behind them. Paul

preached to the Romans (cf. Romans 13:1–7) that obedience to the
government could be viewed as sheer necessity; it could also be seen
as obedience to God in such a way that the Christian could see God
behind even tax collectors. One could take a stance that these were
not bureaucrats, but deacons and liturgical ministers. It did not change
the government nor invest it with any divine rights; it did not even
change the temper and persistence of tax collectors. It made a difference
in the Christian, not in the government.

If the attitude shows up in matters of good citizenship, it also
appears in the New Testament view of family life. The good old Roman
virtues—they were many and solid and their passing was decried by
many a Roman—centered around respect and fidelity and proper po-
sitions within the family. Husbandly love and wifely acceptance of a
role in family life, cherishing of children, obedience by children and
slaves were accepted virtues. The pagan moralists urged them as strongly
as New Testament writers, especially Paul. But the pagan approved
them since there was nothing he could do about a larger society and
its woes (so the Stoics), or because they led to a contented life in which
everyone had a proper place (so the more usual view), or because they
provided the most pleasure for the least effort (so the Hedonists). But
to Paul the reason for living according to accepted custom was that
one was "in Christ" and could grow to spiritual maturity by performing
such actions with a view of becoming like Christ. So in Ephesians
6:5–9 Paul could say, "Slaves, obey your human masters with the
reverence, the awe, and the sincerity you owe to Christ. Do not render
service for appearance only and to please men, but do God's will with
your whole heart as slaves of Christ. Give your service willingly, doing
it for the Lord rather than men. You know that each one, whether
slave or free, will be repaid by the Lord for whatever good he does.
Masters, act in a similar way toward your slaves. Stop threatening
them. Remember that you and they have a Master in heaven who plays
no favorites." The question is not the right or wrong of slavery, but
granted that such was the condition of life, what could one see in it?

Finally, the identifying function of law and custom is strong in
the Bible. The Bible never took the view that one could talk about
doing good and stop there. The standard phrase was, "Walk in the

way of the Lord." One learned God's will with one's feet, not with one's head. To separate understanding from action was derided.

> Happy the man who follows not
> > the counsel of the wicked
> Nor walks in the way of sinners,
> > nor sits in the company of the insolent,
> But delights in the law of the Lord
> > and meditates on his law day and night
> . . . .
> For the Lord watches over the way of the just,
> > but the way of the wicked vanishes.
> > > > Psalm 1:1–2 and 6

Thus the Book of Psalms begins. In the New Testament Christians were first called "those of the Way." (cf. Acts 9:2) They were identified by what they did. If Jews were identified as Jews by dietary and cultic practices, Christians were identified by attendance at the Eucharistic celebration. The fish and the bread became symbols of those who belonged to the Way. The symbols were important because they expressed in a succinct way what people did, not how they argued.

THE SEARCH FOR A PERSON BEHIND THE LAWS

Paying attention to the symbols and images is extremely important to reading the laws of the Bible. It has already been observed in Chapter Two that the Bible is literature and literature conveys its message mainly through images. This is true in the decision-making process which is held out in the Bible as well as in your own decision-making. As noted before, most of our decisions are based on images, not on a rigorous chain of logic. Self-images, the images approved in our society, the images of what our friends and competitors expect, the images of what we would like to be and of what we despise ourselves for being are far more operative in what we do than are the reasons that we usually bring forth after we have made our decisions. The images are not precise, but they do dictate precise actions. Confronted with the need for a decision on how to dress or answer parents, the adolescent male is apt to act out of a *macho* image in an almost predetermined way. The adolescent girl is tempted to follow the behavior of the current heroine. The adults fighting over the back fence will claim that they are arguing about matters of principle, but they are really trying to impose their own images on the neighbors. Politicians are more forthright; they hire public relations people to tailor images for them. It is these images, generic in themselves, which suddenly sharpen into precise determinants of conduct in a specific situation.

If this is the way we function, it is understandable that an adroit author will take advantage of the same technique. For example, the Sermon on the Mount presents a kaleidoscope of pictures. The abstract statement, "You shall not commit murder" is followed by pictures. (cf. Matthew 5:23–24) One of them has a Jew approaching the altar, presumably with his family all around him to offer the usual thanksgiving gifts. It is a joyous scene, but as the action goes forward, he spots his neighbor off in the crowd and remembers the unfinished argument they have been having. Custom would dictate the conventional: pretend the problem is not there. But the man who perceives what "You shall not commit murder" is all about knows that he cannot make a show of coming close to his God while he hates his neighbor. He must put down his gifts, step out of line, and be reconciled with his brother. The precise picture may never be duplicated in our own lives, but it has a powerful impact on us in other circumstances that cannot be determined beforehand. If it were a law, then by some logical process we could go from a general principle to a specific application almost automatically. But it is an image based on the image of God who is perfect and as such it has limitless application.

In citing the commandment about divorce, Matthew's text oddly says that "everyone who divorces his wife . . . forces her to commit adultery" (Matthew 5:32). Now there is no way that any law about divorce can hold a husband responsible for his divorced wife's actions. One must conjure up the scene. The husband has written out the conditions under which he is divorcing his wife and has attended to legal formalities; that is to say, he has protected himself from having his wife make a future claim upon him. Such was the function of the law found in Deuteronomy 24:1. With the stroke of a pen he has cut her off. But what happens to the woman? In the society in which she lived she has no skills or social opportunities to live except to get married again. And those opportunities are limited. She is virtually forced into adultery. That is the sorrowful picture which Matthew intended. It is not a law; it is a vivid picture of the cold, legal husband acting selfishly as contrasted with the God who makes his sun to shine upon both the good and the bad.

It is this conflict between conventional images of action and the biblical presentation that makes the literary aspect succeed so well and that makes us work as readers. The conflict of images is so often there. Matthew cites a saying of Jesus, "He who is not with me is against me." (Matthew 12:30) Mark cites a saying, "Anyone who is not against us is with us." (Mark 9:40) The sayings are going in opposite directions. This is not remarkable since playing off one isolated text against another can often be made to look like a contradiction. What is astonishing is that in Mark the saying is exactly the opposite of what normal instinct would dictate. The apostle John had just presented a problem which the disciples had encountered on their preaching mission: "We saw a man using your name to expel demons and we tried to stop him because he is not of our company." (Mark 9:38) It was the usual common sense of protecting the franchise. But Jesus said, "Do not try to stop him." (Mark 9:39) He then went on to make his apparently broad-minded comment about those who are with us. However, this is followed by an extremely bitter denunciation of those who lead people astray. "It would be better if anyone who leads astray one of these simple believers were to be plunged in the sea with a great millstone fastened around his neck." (Mark 9:42) What is to be said about such disconcerting reverses in instruction? Should one allow false preachers to say and do anything that they want? Or should one protect the innocent? We are left to struggle with the problem.

We shall see more of this in the proverbial sayings and in the parables. It is not an isolated or unusual way for the biblical authors to present their teaching. It may be most disturbing to us. If so, it was intended to be. We often reach our decisions with labored concern since we are pulled back and forth by conflicting images. Should the parent hug the child or spank? Two images are probably fighting, that of the loving and forgiving parent and that of the necessary disciplinarian. No general law can solve the problem; no book on psychology of raising children can give an undoubted answer. In the concrete situation the decision is based on which image of self the parent chooses. The next time he or she may choose the opposite and be equally right—or wrong. The Bible would support either view.

One may imagine a human being who never had such problems, who made all of life's decisions without an internal struggle. Such a person would reach conclusions without doubt, fear, hatred, or love. It would be a simple matter of logic. One may imagine such a person, but it is a stretch of the imagination because we do not ordinarily know persons who act in this way. If we did, we might not know whether to like or dislike them; they would certainly be cold fish. The people we love are an odd mixture, a bundle of contradictions. The ones we remember best are usually eccentric in some way (and then we say that they have character). The ones who are always the same are usually dull and forgettable. It is the *person* who ties together the loose ends of contradiction.

Laws are extremely revelatory, both of the personality of the lawgiver and of what the lawgiver thinks of the subjects. The fearful lawgiver makes many and minute laws, either because he thinks the subjects are incapable of ruling themselves or because he fears them as a threat to his power. The dictator is revealed as a dictator by legal enactments; the ineffective ruler refrains from any lawmaking for fear of being disliked.

So what kind of lawgiver is behind the biblical laws? The really distinctive thing about the Decalog and those other laws in the Old Testament which have been alluded to is that they begin with a simple statement: "I am the Lord." The really distinctive thing about the Sermon on the Mount is that climactic saying: "Be perfect as your heavenly Father is perfect." The really distinctive thing about Paul's ethic is that he leaves his readers to discern God's will for themselves and to act freely on the conviction that Christ lives within them and will tell them what to do. (cf. Romans 12:2) The God of laws trusts his people because he admits that they are like him.

In reading the "do this" sections of the Bible, you must always be alert for the final truth which lies behind the text. As the Bible sees it, it is the emerging image of God within each of us which is challenged and challenging. The image is emerging through a confusion of darker images which are also a part of us. The final word is not a simple "Do precisely this and you will be justified," but rather "Seek first the kingdom of God." (Matthew 6:33; Luke 12:31)

FIVE

Reading Reflective Passages in the Bible

THE PLACE OF REFLECTIVE MATERIAL
IN THE BIBLE

Student preachers today are often told to think of a sermon as a story. This is not a ploy to get them to tell more stories—though that might be helpful—but to understand that a sermon, like a story, reveals character. It may reveal a con man or a struggling human being; it may tell the story of a coldly intellectual person or it may be a story of confusion, laziness, and so on. The most immediate reaction of the hearers will not be to the logic of the thought, but a simple "I like that person" or the disturbing contrary. If the sermon is to do us much good, it must also play into our character development as we are set thinking about our own story. All of this is difficult work for both parties since, despite the similitude, a sermon is still not a story. We can get wrapped up in a story for hours at a time, but we want our sermons short.

The Bible has much sermon material, gratefully short. The Book of Deuteronomy is built on a framework of five sermons which are put into the mouth of Moses; the Gospel of Matthew is hung together on a pattern of five sermons which Jesus preached. 1 Peter is most likely a catechetical instruction for converts before Baptism; James seems to be short notes for five sermons on wisdom themes. The prophetic books are usually made up of short synopses of various preachings of the prophets. We shall not, however, consider prophetic preaching in this chapter; the prophet as poet is more important for me.

After sermons we can list many passages which can with some stretching of the term be called essays. The passages I refer to come in all sizes from one-liners such as proverbs to developed essays such as the Epistle to the Hebrews. Somewhat akin to this are letters of instruction. The Old Testament has some of these; for example, the letter which Jeremiah wrote to his compatriots after the fall of Jerusalem instructing them to remain faithful (cf. Jeremiah 29:1–23). The best known of such correspondence is, of course, the Epistles which are traditionally called "of Paul."

THE REFLECTIVE MOOD

The catalog given above is very brief and partial, but it will serve our purpose of asking what is behind the vast amount of reflective writing in the Bible. As a starting point which is helpful but by no means certain, let us take the centuries between 500 B.C. and the first century B.C. Much of the writing in this period is centered on what we call "wisdom" for want of a better name. A large amount of it was associated with the study of the Torah or Law. How important this was and how it functioned can be briefly glimpsed in a few words from the finale of a beautiful lyric poem which Jesus ben Sirach wrote shortly after 200 B.C. The subject of the poem is wisdom.

> He who eats of me will hunger still,
>   he who drinks of me will thirst for more;
> He who obeys me will not be put to shame,
>   he who serves me will never fail.
> All this is true of the book of the Most High's covenant,
>   the law which Moses commanded us
>   as an inheritance for the community of Jacob.
>   Sirach 24:20–22

This attitude of putting the Law first as the subject of reflection carried over into Christian times. The Sermon on the Mount focuses on what Jesus meant by "fulfilling" the Law. The later writers of the New Testament substituted Jesus for the Law as a subject of meditation. Luke makes the point several times in his Infancy Narrative that Mary kept all these things concerning Jesus in her heart, and that is a proper biblical way of saying that she meditated about them. The writings of Paul are the result of much community and personal reflection on the meaning of the Christ event. One of Paul's most frequent prayers is for wisdom.

We may well ask what this meditation consisted of. Jesus once told a story about the prudent man who brings out of his storehouse things both new and old. Much of the meditating was recalling the events of old; whether ancient in the case of the Old Testament, or more recent in the case of the New Testament makes little difference. The "new" was the discovery of new meanings for these old stories.

The earliest post-Christian Jewish commentators we know of were the rabbis. They developed a system of interpretation which was curiously part hardnosed realism and part unfettered spiritual vision. The words of each text had to be the exact words (and so they developed an almost incredible skill at preserving the text) and the words had to have a precise meaning. But once this was done, the words could be used as bridges to other texts which might have nothing substantial to do with the first. Key phrases in stories spun off into similar key words in totally different stories. The mind went on creating bridges between events past, present, and hoped for, between ordinances which were quite apart in their original setting but applied to one present problem. The later Christian writers were inclined to do the same thing by using symbols as the bridging element. It is not a method which our present scholars encourage, but at its best moments it did free the mind for daring insights into connectives between the new and the old which no formalized or scientific logic can achieve.

Another type of reflective method can be seen in the proverbs. A proverb can quite comfortably stand alone; it may have no surrounding context. Yet writers do not sit down in the secrecy of their rooms to think up proverbs. The proverb arises out of much community living.

The ways of acting of many generations have been observed; the good and the bad, the successful and the unsuccessful have been sorted out. This has been put into words, reflected upon by many, modified, and the tentative words savored to their fullest before the final saying emerged.

> The man of violent temper pays the penalty;
>> even if you rescue him, you will have to do it again.
>>> Proverbs 19:19

We observe in our conversations that quoting a proverb tends to end the discussion. All the discussion has gone before the stating of the proverb. We may pause to consider how the proverb has summarized the conversation, but unless we are willing to go back and challenge the saying, there is not much more discussion possible. The same is true of many of the sayings of Paul which are proverb-like. He has a genius for the quotable quote. "To me to live is Christ" (Philippians 1:21); "Since we live by the spirit, let us follow the spirit's lead" (Galatians 5:25); "There are in the end three things that last: faith, hope, and love, and the greatest of these is love." (1 Corinthians 13:13) They can cap any discussion. Yet many of them are deliberately provocative. "God's folly is wiser than men, and his weakness more powerful than men." (1 Corinthians 1:25) All of them arise from much reflection and, apparently, much discussion among Christians. Unless we are willing to challenge and go back to the prior discussion, we miss much of what was intended. We can read only a little of such material at one time; we must find the saying that triggers our minds to explore the experience which is both in the saying and in our lives. Such reading is preferably done with many pauses.

TECHNIQUES AND FUNCTIONS OF SERMONS

A closer look at the techniques of composing sermons, essays, and letters—insofar as we can discern them—will be helpful for understanding something of the function which these writings were intended to have and of how they may affect us. First, as to sermons, it has been noted that they rely heavily on a remembering of past events. Remember is a key word in the Bible, often used, and decisive in shaping a people, whether Jewish or Christian. It was the takeoff point for most sermonizing. The remembering, however, was not a rote recital of what everybody already knew. It was used to apply ancient experience to new situations and often to introduce startlingly new directions.

For example, the first lengthy sermon in the Bible is the speech of Moses at the beginning of the Book of Deuteronomy, 1:6 to 4:40. A preliminary note says that Moses began to explain the Law, but there is very little of legal comment in the sermon except a strong admonition to avoid idolatry. The sermon itself begins with a lengthy recalling of what had happened to the Israelites since they had left Horeb. The adventures involved in the first attempts to organize the people, the ill-fated attack on Canaan from the Negeb, the wandering in the desert and the peaceful journey through Edom, Moab, and Ammon are sketched until the decisive victories over Sehon and Og are won. Along the way Moses explains rather wistfully that he himself would not be allowed to enter the Promised Land because he had shared some of the doubts.

Such remembering might function in many ways: as a legal basis for conquest, as an assertion of Moses' right to leadership, as an exhortation to further conquest, and so on. However, as the sermon goes on it becomes apparent that the story has a different center of gravity. The first point is made near the middle of the sermon: "For what god in heaven or on earth can perform deeds as mighty as yours?" (Deuteronomy 3:24) The deeds which appear so difficult for humans are made to appear as quite normal when done by God. Twice the action begins almost casually; in Deuteronomy 1:6 God says, "You have stayed long enough at this mountain." The fears of the unknown are dispelled by the closeness of a familiar God. "What great nation is there that has gods so close to it as the LORD, our God, is to us whenever we call upon him?" (Deuteronomy 4:7) God is described as a jealous God; he abhors any idolatry in this land which he is giving to them. So serious is this threat that if they give in to worshipping any other god, the Lord will scatter them among the nations. Yet he is also a merciful

God and even then they shall not be able to escape him: "Yet there too you shall seek the LORD, your God." (Deuteronomy 4:29)

All of this has already happened; all of it is to happen again. The remembering is also the hoping. Such a sermon might be in season at almost any time. It is put in the mouth of Moses before the people crossed the Jordan to face the far more terrifying armies that awaited them there. The final text of the sermon, however, dates to the time of the Babylonian Exile some eight centuries later and functions as an encouragement not to abandon the ancient religion however much it is derided in that foreign land. The exiled people must not be discouraged, however evident is the justice of the punishment they are receiving. The meaning of a jealous but merciful God has become so much deeper.

This pattern of remembering the past to confront the present is repeated regularly and was understood by the hearers. Jeremiah 25:1–13 is often called the Temple Sermon and represents fairly well what Jeremiah's message was all about. Its point is a plaintive cry to turn back. As so often the people are called upon to remember the land which the Lord had given to their fathers. This extremely common expression is no chauvinistic appeal to territorial integrity, but a call to realize that the land is a living thing which can be cared for and nurtured only when its God is worshipped within it. So also the threat of punishment is put in territorial terms—the avenger from the north and the seventy years of captivity in Babylon. The sermon is only a few verses long, but it is clear that the starting point is the remembrance of the past and the conclusion is that it was a biting criticism of the present. Nobody had to explain that to the priests and royal officials who heard Jeremiah; they carted him off to jail and accused him of treason.

The same thing can be seen in such New Testament sermons as those in the Acts of the Apostles. In the first recorded sermon of Paul to a Jewish audience in Antioch of Pisidia (cf. Acts 13:16–41), the beginning is a reference to the sojourn in Egypt, the Exodus, the period of the Judges, David, and Solomon. Paul then switches to more recent history as he recounts the preaching of John the Baptist and the passion, death, and resurrection of Jesus. This is followed by citations of texts from the Old Testament illustrating that the Messiah was to be incorruptible. Such a sermon can be very brief since the hearers already know the story and believe deeply in it. Paul tried a parallel approach with pagans at the Areopagus in Athens. He began by remarking that he had seen an altar there to "the unknown god"; then he went on to a traditional Greek concept that the gods had allotted times and places to all peoples, cited the Greek poet to the effect that we are all the offspring of the gods, and finally zeroed in on Jesus who was surely such a one since he had been raised from the dead. Apparently the Athenians were not as impressed by their own traditions as the Jews were; the discourse did not even result in a riot. At any rate, the technique of sermonizing in the Bible is to recall the past, emphasize the total initiative of God, and then call for complete dependence on him in some present circumstance.

The profit in knowing something of the technique is that it may provide the clues for understanding what the sermon is all about. The remembrance of the past is not done for the historian's purpose of getting the facts exact nor for the apologist's purpose of making them prove something. This is the tendency of much of modern commentary on such sermons. In the biblical preacher's technique, the events are often compressed, rearranged, or even romanticized. For example, in the sermon of Moses at the beginning of Deuteronomy, it appears that the kind of idolatry being denounced has been shaded in the direction of the Babylonian pantheism instead of the older pagan worship of Canaan. An extreme form of such sermonizing can be found in what is called *midrash*. *Midrash* takes off from some event in the past, tends to key in on a specific word, and then develops a totally new application. In the very late Book of the Wisdom of Solomon (about 75 B.C.) the nine concluding chapters seem to retell the story of the Exodus in a poetic way. Yet the author is not really speaking of the Egypt of the time of Moses; he is speaking of the persecutions which the Alexandrian Jews of his own time were undergoing. He uses the ancient stories and images, then makes them into an exhortation for contemporary Jews.

> When they determined to put to death
>   the infants of the holy ones,

and when a single boy had been cast forth but saved (viz. Moses),
As a reproof you carried off their multitude of sons
and made them perish all at once in the mighty water (viz. the
Reed Sea).
That night was known beforehand to our fathers, (viz. the Passover)
that, with sure knowledge of the oaths in which they put their
faith,
they might have courage.
Your people awaited the salvation of the just
and the destruction of their foes.

Wisdom 18:5–7

The details of the Plagues, the night of the Passover, and the drowning
of Pharaoh's soldiers in the Reed Sea get mixed up in this remembering,
but it conveys a rather bloodcurdling hope of salvation and then an
extremely deep new insight into faith. The discourse had begun with
the saying:

But you, our God, are good and true,
slow to anger, and governing all with mercy.
For even if we sin, we are yours, and know your might;
but we will not sin, knowing that we belong to you.
For to know you well is complete justice,
and to know your might is the root of immortality.

Wisdom 15:1–3

PROVERBS AND OTHER SUCH WRITING

The key to reading proverbs is to find the hidden question. On
the surface the proverb is simply an observation of the way in which
people act. "A mild answer calms wrath, but a harsh word stirs up
anger." (Proverbs 15:1) It is a saying coined from experience; it may
suggest action, but in itself it is not an ethical imperative and it often
has nothing religious about it. Whether one should calm wrath remains
an unanswered question. The too obvious proverb becomes a cliche.
"He who betrays a secret cannot be trusted, he will never find an

intimate friend." (Sirach 27:16) The Bible never quite reaches the heights of banality such as we have in some of our sayings: "The game is never over until the last out is made," or "Nice guys don't win," or that perfect example pronounced by the late mayor of Chicago: "The future is ahead of us." Yet there are bad proverbs as well as good ones in the Bible.

The easiest form of proverb is the "better-than" type. "Better a dish of herbs where love is than a fatted ox and hatred with it." (Proverbs 15:17) "It is better to dwell in a corner of the housetop than in a roomy house with a quarrelsome woman." (Proverbs 21:9) Almost as easy is the "happy he who" saying. "Happy the man who follows not the counsel of the wicked." (Psalm 1:1) "Happy the man who finds wisdom, the man who gains understanding" (Proverbs 3:13), or "Happy are the poor in spirit; the reign of God is theirs." (Matthew 5:3) Both of these rely on simple comparisons, expressed or implied. Good comparisons do reveal much shrewdness and convey deep emotions. "Lion's prey are the wild asses of the desert; so too the poor are feeding grounds for the rich." (Sirach 13:18) The negative comparison, the antithesis, is the real salt of biblical proverbs. "The bread of deceit is sweet to a man, but afterwards his mouth will be filled with gravel." (Proverbs 20:17)

The unthinking acceptance of proverbs is itself satirized by Koheleth. Every language has a saying which prefers a good name to something else which is considered good. "A good name is more desirable than great riches" (Proverbs 22:1) is one biblical version. Koheleth stands it on its head:

> A good name is better than good ointment,
>> and the day of death than the day of birth.
>>> Koheleth 7:1

The "happy he who . . ." sayings get made into paradoxes which challenge all sane thinking. "Blest are you poor . . . Blest are you who hunger . . . Blest are you who are weeping . . . Blest shall you be when men hate you . . ." (Luke 6:20–22) To miss the biting and astringent antithesis is to ignore the function which they had. They are not sugar-coated sayings promising reward to the pious, but challenges to all conventional thinking.

This same sting is found in parables. Parables are very close to proverbs. Luke 14:7 reads: "He (Jesus) went on to address a parable to the guests, noticing how they were trying to get the places of honor at the table." What follows, however, is not a story, but an instruction centering on a proverb which is stated in verse 11: "For everyone who exalts himself shall be humbled and he who humbles himself shall be exalted." There is nothing new or even religious about this saying or about the whole passage; it is simply observation on manners and it has been said innumerable times before and after. It gets its bite from the context insofar as Jesus confronted these guests with their boorish conduct. But there is more. "Whenever you give a lunch or dinner, do not invite your friends or brothers or relatives or wealthy neighbors. They might invite you in return and thus repay you. No, when you have a reception, invite beggars and the crippled, the lame and the blind." (Luke 14:12–13) That is fairly outrageous, but one of the in-group of Pharisees who was present made the unctious "happy he who . . ." remark: "Happy is he who eats bread in the kingdom of God." (Luke 14:15) That provoked Jesus into relating what we would really consider a parable, the story of the banquet which all the invited guests spurned. In the circumstances of self-complacent guests who considered themselves happy to be eating bread in God's kingdom, the story was anything but pious and consoling.

In reading parables the problem is not to clarify the small details which make them realistic in the culture in which they were spoken, but to search out the items which make them unrealistic. The sower went out to sow his seed and some fell among rocks and some on a footpath and some among thorns and some on good ground which yielded various harvests. The problem is not to learn about Palestinian agricultural methods but to ask: What farmer would be so foolish as to do his planting in this way? Another farmer had his good crop ruined by an enemy who sowed weeds among it; his solution was simply to let both grow until the harvest and then reap the weeds before the good grain. Realistically this is absurd; it can't be done in

Palestine or anywhere else. Then there is the story of the mustard seed which grew so big that all the birds preferred to roost in its branches rather than in trees. All of these stories are in the thirteenth chapter of Matthew and all of them turn conventional ways of acting upside down. Nor are they explained. The final parable in that series is simply: "The reign of God is like yeast which a woman took and kneaded into three measures of flour. Eventually the whole mass of dough began to rise." (Matthew 13:33) That is all there is and you are left with a puzzle. Scarcely less puzzling is the teacher's explanation of why he told stories like this. "I use parables when I speak to them because they look but do not see, they listen but do not hear or understand." (Matthew 13:13) The parable is indeed a mystery and that is why it is so dynamic in developing thought.

The essays have something of the same technique about them. The writers of proverbs (or perhaps more often the collectors) put together sayings on various topics; honesty in business, fidelity, and hard work (or the lack of it)—such were some of their favorite topics. Such proverbs, all on one topic, tended to form sections by themselves. But there were passages, sometimes very ancient, which had been such mini-essays from the beginning. The Sayings of Agur in Proverbs 30:1-6 (or 1-4) form a connected discourse on who can know the mysteries of God, and they appear to have been in that format long before most of the rest of the book was written. The beginning of the text is a confession: "I am not God." Then the questioning begins: Who has known God? Who is his son? Who has gone up into heaven? Who, in effect, can know or control life? The final word in the text is that there is no final word. Only this is said, "Add nothing to his words, lest he reprove you, and you be exposed as a deceiver." It was the endless quest of these writers to assault the frontiers of understanding, to fall back before the immensity of the mystery, and then to try again.

To say that such an essay leads into mystery is not to say that it goes nowhere. The sayings of ben Sirach are often prosaic, but he sometimes breaks out of this into sublime and challenging poetry. Chapter 42:15 to 43:35 is a good example of a great lyric poem on nature and its God.

> Now will I recall God's works;
>> what I have seen, I will describe.
>>> Sirach 42:15

There follows a litany of praise for God who knows all and who made the sun, the moon, the stars, the rainbow, the lightning, the thunder, the snow, the dripping clouds, and the sea. It is playful as well as beautiful. Then ben Sirach makes his point:

> More than this we need not add;
>> let the last word be, he is all in all.
> Let us praise him the more, since we cannot fathom him,
>> for greater is he than all his works.
> Awful indeed is the LORD'S majesty,
>> and wonderful is his power.
> Lift up your voices to glorify the LORD,
>> though he is still beyond your power to praise;
> Extol him with renewed strength,
>> and weary not, though you cannot reach the end:
> For who can see him and describe him?
>> or who can praise him as he is?
> Beyond these, many things lie hid;
>> only a few of his words have we seen.
> It is the LORD who has made all things,
>> and to those who fear him he gives wisdom.
>>> Sirach 43:28–35

THE EPISTLES

The Epistles of Paul are much in this tradition. Great effort has been expended to define the literary form of Paul's Epistles in order to have a surer means of interpretation. The quest has not been highly successful. Paul surely did not compose his thoughts with topic sentences and paragraphs and developmental points as we are taught to do in school. Neither did he write in the orderly fashion of the classic rhetoricians of Rome or Greece. What we can discern is that he marshalled his ideas and images around general topics somewhat in the fashion of the proverb groupings.

The most frequently used technique of Paul is to tie together his passages by catchwords which express strong antitheses: life and death, sin and justice, faith and works, spirit and flesh, wisdom and folly, law and freedom—the list can go on extensively. These are techniques which were used in the later sapiential writings of the Old Testament; Paul was an heir to that literary as well as religious tradition. He was also an heir to that earthy and concrete approach to life which was far more satisfied with finding a hard fact which revealed something of life than any number of theories. His preference is for the concrete word even if it is a flagrant assault on the senses. Hence words and ideas which appear in our translations (and in our tradition) as abstractions must be understood in a much more concrete and experiential way.

I Corinthians is an almost defiant manifesto against any other view. "Since in God's wisdom the world did not come to know him through 'wisdom,' it pleased God to save those who believe through the absurdity of the preaching of the gospel. Yes, Jews demand 'signs' and Greeks look for 'wisdom,' but we preach Christ crucified—a stumbling block to Jews, and an absurdity to Gentiles; but to those who are called, Jews and Greeks alike, Christ the power of God and the wisdom of God. For God's folly is wiser than men, and his weakness more powerful than men." (1 Corinthians 1:21–25)

It is a good example of Paul's technique and points out what you should expect in reading Paul. "Christ crucified"—Paul could not have chosen a more barbaric expression; it was crass, brutal, and disgusting. He could have put it much more acceptably in abstract terms—salvation through reconciliation or something of that sort. But that is exactly what he rejects; it must be the brutal picture, a malefactor dying on a cross. That was the connection with reality and it was with reality that Paul began. Nor should the other terms be read differently. The "wisdom" of the Greeks is no abstraction; Paul had talked to the professional scholars in Athens and they had snubbed him; there is passion and repudiation of the experience in Paul's words. The absurdity of the preaching of the Gospel is no mere phrase dreamed up by a public relations man; Paul could see himself in synagogues and market-places being jeered and dodging rocks. The stumbling block to the

Jews was not a clever phrase thought up on the spur of the moment;
it was an ancient picture from a Psalm in which the king of Judah had
been scorned by the other kings of a pagan coalition and yet had
emerged as the hero. Christ used the same passage with telling irony
in confronting his opponents (cf. Matthew 21:42) and they realized
immediately that he was talking about them as the stumbling block.
To be "called" was not a theological abstraction; every Jew knew
precisely what he was called in that pagan society. It meant to be a
people set apart in cities and towns as well as in God's plans. The folly
of God and the weakness of God are not just a brilliant paradox; they
conjure up immediately the whole conflict of Jerusalem and Athens,
the ancient meditation on the Law and the rational attempt of philosophers to explain the world and of philosopher kings to keep some
control over it. There is a breathless crescendo to these sayings which
pit so many conflicting ideas against one another.

It is also the Christian experience, Paul's as well as that of his
hearers and of us. Like experience, it is not neatly arranged. The first
four chapters of this Epistle keep coming back to the same ideas, now
from one point of experience and now from another. In reading Paul
you must look for these strong antitheses, follow them down through
many variations, and try to grasp the shape of the whole starkly realistic
picture. Reading one verse of Paul is as dangerous as citing one horn
of a dilemma; erecting one statement into an abstract principle is even
more precarious. The whole flow of a wise man's thought as it grapples
with unspeakable mystery must be grasped. Paul himself said that he
couldn't put into words the things he had seen.

The Epistles of John follow something of the same pattern. The
first Epistle keeps circling around a central thought of the reality and
indestructibility of love. John attacks the problem from several
angles—rejecting all self-serving ideas of love as pretty or self-fulfilling,
asserting the indefectibility of God's love and the need for practical
action toward others on our part. "The man without love has known
nothing of God, for God is love." (1 John 4:8) The phrase I have just
quoted stands in marked contrast to my own abstract summary of the
Epistle; the one is conventional Western logic, the other is Semitic
realism.

SUMMARY

No summary can really be given for the chapter you have just read. Some things, however, stand out. There are large sections of the Bible which must be approached with a reflective mood, a willingness to read little and to think much, to let the mind explore on its own the images and experiences which have been presented. It is the concrete experience or image which matters; abstractions should be eschewed as much as possible. The flow of the thought is in a circular direction rather than in a straight line from A to Z. The progress is by antithesis and paradox more than by putting together building blocks to form a neat structure. The major tenets of Christianity, incidentally, are all paradoxes. Behind the most obvious and consoling saying, you should suspect a twist which will land you upside down to see life from a completely new angle. The function of the whole is not to provide you with convenient prepackaged conclusions but to lead you into mystery. There is little of problem-solving; there is much of thought-provoking and that on a level which we rarely reach on our own.

Commentaries are of great help in defining words, marking out groups of sayings which are to be taken as a unit, clarifying concepts which have been taken over from earlier parts of the Bible or that were current in that world. The scholars are also very helpful in establishing the principal themes which rule various sections of the reflective writings. However, you should be aware that centuries of Christian theology have imposed systems of thought on material which never aimed in the direction of systematic thought. As a matter of cultural tradition in our Western world, we Greeks still seek wisdom whether from computers or from scientific study. We often get so deeply immersed in our own needs, and so intrigued with our own tools of the trade, that we overlook what is really being sought. We coined the phrase that nature abhors a vacuum; we tend to think that we should also abhor a mystery. It helps us every once in a while to admit that we simply do not know what a particular biblical passage means or that we see only a small part of the meaning.

SIX

Understanding the Psalms

HOW WE USE THE PSALMS

The Book of Psalms forms a particularly rich part of our religious heritage. It is sometimes the only part of the Old Testament with which people are familiar. Protestants seem comfortable with the Psalms as private prayers and meditations; Catholics of all sorts (and there are different rites) are more accustomed to meet the Psalms in their liturgies; the whole Christian heritage shares many songs in common which are based on the Psalms. The Jewish congregations, of course, continue to make great use of them as they have for centuries since the times of the Jerusalem Temple. And they have a story to tell even older than that.

> Give to the LORD, you sons of God,
>   give to the LORD glory and praise,
> Give to the LORD the glory due his name;
>   adore the LORD in holy attire.
> Psalm 29:1–2

Except for the distinctive name Lord or Yahweh, the Psalm seems to go back to a pre-Israelite song used by the ancient Canaanites. One

can well imagine some lonely temple perched on a mountain above the
sea in which the pagan priests chanted:

> The voice of the LORD is over the waters.
>> the God of glory thunders,
>> the LORD, over vast waters.
> The voice of the LORD is mighty;
>> the voice of the Lord is majestic.
> The voice of the LORD breaks the cedars,
>> the LORD breaks the cedars of Lebanon.
>
> Psalm 29:3–5

The cadence is the same as hymns from Ras Shamra in Lebanon; the
idea of god presiding over the chaos of the sea is familiar. It would
seem that the Israelites had stolen the hymn and the whole idea of
praising God as the presider over the unruly universe from their pagan
predecessors. Later the early Christians adapted the Psalms for their
own worship.

In approaching the Psalms in this way we are emphasizing the
continuity and the self-identification of a people. It is a thought to
which we must return later. Suffice it to say that these are essentially
songs for a people, the expression in community of their belief in the
kind of God whom they worship.

THE PSALMS AS POETRY

Study of the Psalms in the past century has centered on the use
of them in the Jewish cult. Almost all Psalms were written to be sung
in a community worship setting. All of them eventually were so used
and there is evidence that the entire Book of Psalms has at least five
separate collections which are still set off by doxologies or concluding
verses which proclaim the blessedness of praising God. There are also
indications that some of the collections belonged to named choirs such
as the Sons of Korah, Asaph, etc. Some of the Psalms have musical
directions given before the first verse. The Psalter was a choir collection
early on.

Modern study of the Psalms has concentrated on the patterns which were used to create their structure. To simplify the scholar's conclusion greatly, Psalms are grouped as hymns of praise or thanksgiving, laments, blessings, and so on. The study proceeded from an analysis of the literary form of Psalms rather than from what they said. It was noticed that the hymns of praise usually begin with an introductory statement such as: "Praise the Lord," "Sing a new song to the Lord," "Rejoice in the Lord," and so forth. After the invocation a simple pattern is developed, praise the Lord as the Creator of the world or as the Lord of history.

The hymn might be long or short; it might be pure or mingled with other forms; but it was consistent enough to dictate that some cultic action appropriate to the text must have gone with it. Some hymns were seen to demand a ceremony for the enthronement of Yahweh as the Great King; some were appropriate for a New Year ceremony for God the Creator; a parallel group were appropriate for the enthronement ceremony of a reigning king or a commemorative ceremony of that act. Thanksgivings and laments manifested their own patterns and demanded their own life settings in the cult.

Unfortunately, it was discovered as the study proceeded that few of the Psalms followed the scholar's diagnosis exactly. Some hymns are written in the form which we decided is the norm. But most of them are too free to be confined within a set pattern. One can continue to subdivide forms until all the Psalms have been accounted for, but this destroys the utility which ordinary users have for quick understandings. On the other hand, the study did inadvertently uncover something more valuable.

It will be noticed that the words the scholars used for their classifications all represent feelings. A result which was not intended must be important. The basic mood behind praise and thanks is one of awe for the mighty deeds and words of God. The function of such prayer is not to give a logical or elaborate explanation of God, but simply to praise the mystery which is seen. And this passes over into simple wonder and praise for the creature whom God has created.

O LORD, our LORD,
　　how glorious is your name over all the earth!
When I behold your heavens, the work of your fingers,
　　the moon and the stars which you set in place—
What is man that you should be mindful of him,
　　or the son of man that you should care for him?
You have made him little less than the angels,
　　and crowned him with glory and honor.
Psalm 8:2 and 4–6

The mood of lament is one which quickly passes over to that of an unshakable confidence and sense of security. The sudden change in mood is needed to make the security emerge.

For his anger lasts but a moment;
　　a lifetime, his good will.
At nightfall, weeping enters in
　　but with the dawn, rejoicing.
Psalm 30:6

Perhaps it may be simpler for us in our task to deal with the Psalms as poetry in the same way that we deal with any poetry. This too has some limitations which we should note before we become too committed. First of all, poetry suffers from translation more than any other form of written communication. The metre, the rhyme, and even the rhythm are lost in the hands of a clumsy translator and transmuted into something different in the hands of a sensitive one. The sound of words, the connotations which are conjured up, the soul-stirring traditions behind them are largely lost or at least changed for a foreigner. The Star-Spangled Banner might sound better in Russian, but it would not be the Star-Spangled Banner. Fortunately, most modern translations of the Bible have printed a good amount of the prophetic literature in the poetic format which we are accustomed to using and an attempt has been made to capture the original vigor. Still, we suffer severe limitations in this field.

Then there are the more common problems of reading any poetry. The first reading of a poem, except the most simplistic, may leave us saying: What was that all about? The prose writer has a simple criterion: be so clear that you cannot be misunderstood. The poet seems to ignore this and deliberately aims to stretch us to the utmost. Strange words and strange places for words seem to be the order of poetic writing. The problem is not that the poet wants to be misunderstood, but that he or she wants to concentrate such an intensity of feeling into such a space as will explode the reader's mind. That sentence itself, although in prose, requires some "unpacking", to use our current cliche, but it does not contain any great amount of feeling. It is simply prose.

The poet's first objective is to convey an intense feeling. "The LORD is my shepherd" is a well-known poem from the Psalms. (cf. Psalm 23) It appeals because it conveys an intense feeling of comfort and security. The pictures it uses are quieting—"verdant pastures," "restful waters," "the overflowing cup," "the anointing oil," "the house of the Lord." The only negative is denied entrance: "Even though I walk in the dark valley I fear no evil; for you are at my side."

Mood or the conveying of an intense feeling is the key to understanding poetry. The effect of any Psalm must be grasped from the total feeling which is conveyed, not from the individual statements or pictures which are used. So we may be shocked by the Psalmist's prayer against the Babylonians.

> O daughter of Babylon, you destroyer,
>   happy the man who shall repay you the evil you have done
>   us!
> Happy the man who shall seize and smash
>   your little ones against the rock!
>
>   Psalm 137:8–9

It is rather bloodcurdling and base, though no more so than the parallel curses against Babylon in the Book of Revelation. Yet this is not the mood of the Psalm prayer. The mood is a plaintive cry for God to act. Enslaved, scorned, and dejected in Babylon, the people were taunted to sing to a God who seemed powerless outside his own territory. The doubt nagged even the most pious.

> How could we sing a song to the LORD
>   in a foreign land?
>   Psalm 137:4

Someone had the courage to say the unspeakable. Out of that trauma arose a deep feeling of commitment.

> If I forget you, Jerusalem
>   may my right hand be forgotten!
> May my tongue cleave to my palate
>   if I remember you not,
>   if I place not Jerusalem ahead of my joy.
>   Psalm 137:5—6

It is this alternation of light and darkness, of moods of somber despair and unrestrained joy which make the biblical prayers realistic and which makes them speak to our moods.

Mood is, indeed, a subjective thing. There are phrases which strike us as fair and bright and all inclusive at one moment and which later become pedestrian for us. The text remains the text but our mood has changed and we no longer need that one.

GUIDELINES

It is not all subjective. The understanding of the Psalm poem does have some guidelines which govern the kind of subjective mood which we are expected to experience. The indicators of direction are the structure, the images, the tension and finally the mood.

The structure conforms generically to the forms which the scholars have diagnosed. In some of our English translations of the Bible we have written into the printed text various titles which tell us that this is a hymn, a prayer, a petition, or a lament, etc. We may also have the text divided into blocks of material with numbers to indicate where the various divisions or changes of direction occur. These are helpful. The trick, however, is to appreciate that the structure is going somewhere. Hymns often begin with an invitation to praise God and then end with a similar reprise. This is a wrap-up technique. Laments often begin with a cry for help and then recapitulate the note of confidence at the end.

The images are most important since poetry usually works its spell by creating pictures. It is a rare Psalm which expresses itself in abstract terms. For great poetry it is the basic things of life which are used as images. Often they connect immediately with a long tradition which can be summoned up simply by mentioning a single word. So "father", "king", "Temple", "the Law" are used to create pictures instantaneously. Oddly enough we respond to many such words even though we no longer have any actual experience of them. "The Lord is my shepherd" means something to us although most of us have probably never seen a shepherd and rarely a sheep. The gathering-in of the sheaves appeals to us even though we have never done it. Images within individual Psalms tend to center around a common theme. There will be images of warriors, swords, shields, high places to defend, rocks, etc. in one Psalm; sun, moon, stars, rain, snow, etc. in another; perjurers, liars, implacable enemies, back-biters, etc. in a third.

As in stories, it usually takes some tension to make a good poem. There are some joyful hymns which speak only of the grandeur and goodness of God. But it must be remembered that such poems were sung defiantly in the face of the surrounding pagans who did not believe it. Most of the Psalms have a high level of tension within them between those who walk in the Way of the Lord and the fools who do not, between the pious and the impious who want to kill them, between the God of Order and the Chaos of the world. Laments are the most numerous by type in the Psalter; they always have a high level of tension between the trials which the Psalmist (and Psalm singer) experiences and the hoped-for deliverance which comes just in the nick of time.

Out of all of this comes the mood or feeling. We cannot dictate what feeling the hearer should get from any individual Psalm—that is truly subjective. But we can say from our previous considerations that we know something about the direction in which the text is leading us.

SELF-IDENTIFICATION

The dominant mood which the Psalms seem to create is one of
security and serenity. Peace, confidence, joy abound in the majority
of Psalms. The lament which leaves us lamenting is rare indeed; only
one or two Psalms, such as Psalm 88, leave us unrescued. Several
Psalms which are largely meditative leave us with a mood of bewilderment. But these are exceptions which emphasize one phase of what
the singing of Psalms was intended to accomplish. In their original
settings or in their final biblical use in the post-exilic Temple (after
500 B.C. roughly) the Psalms were an exsultant proclamation of the
power of God to protect this Chosen People. The Psalter had its note
of triumphalism, but it was a mature triumphalism which could still
take into itself the hurt and the bewilderment of some human experiences.

We are all familiar with school songs, company songs and most
of all with patriotic songs. What such songs do most effectively is to
give us a sense of belonging. They separate between "them" and "us"
in a legitimate way. They also tell something important about the
basic beliefs which hold us together. "My country 'tis of thee, sweet
land of liberty" or "America the Beautiful" are proclamations of our
faith. In a similar way Israelites were identified as Israelites in the time
of the first Temple as the people who went up to Jerusalem several
times a year for great celebrations and sang songs to a different God
called Yahweh. The songs identified them as people who believed they
had been chosen to do this, that they had received promises through
Father Abraham, that their God dwelt in this city Jerusalem, that he
was all-mighty and merciful, and that he was leading them to a new
age. The songs they wrote identified what kind of people they were.

Out of the feeling created by the images, however, emerges an
insight, not simply a pleasant sensation. Public speakers are sometimes
urged to "put a little more feeling in your speeches." The insight is
there but it gets lost. The poet starts with the feeling; sometimes in
inferior poetry the idea is not all that worthwhile and we have simply
an overly sentimental and sickly sweet confection. The true poem bursts

on us, fresh and vivid in its insight. Poets are sometimes considered the madmen of the universe. They see the world in a totally different perspective from other people. They are not selling a new brand of toothpaste or a formula for a microcomputer; their ideas are truly earth-shaking. Out of the word-smithing and the intensity of feeling which is always localized in concrete images comes an insight which somehow disturbs us all. Macbeth says near the end of the play when all of his ambitious schemes have collapsed:

> Tomorrow, and tomorrow, and tomorrow,
> Creeps in this petty pace from day to day,
> To the last syllable of recorded time;
> And all our yesterdays have lighted fools
> The way to dusty death. Out, out, brief candle;
> Life's but a walking shadow; a poor player,
> That struts and frets his hour upon the stage,
> And then is heard no more; it is a tale
> Told by an idiot, full of sound and fury,
> Signifying nothing.

The defeat of Macbeth is total; it is not just his plans to reign as king which are defeated, but the life of all of us. The dramatic impact could not have been achieved with abstractions; Shakespeare had to create this scene of vivid images to bring the idea home. Yet the idea is so much larger than the scene.

One final remark of a more pedestrian nature needs to be made here. Poetry abounds in specifics—names of people and places, objects, customs, and those more subtle nuances of language. You can no more read biblical prophecy without some aid than you can read the *Divina Comedia* of Dante cold. The locale and the situation of prophecy must be set with some precision. Often we can only do it in a general way, but that much is helpful. An adequate commentary is very necessary; even the short introductions and footnotes which most Bibles provide should be read carefully.

SEVEN

Reading the Prophets

THE CHALLENGE OF POETRY

Most of the prophetic writing in the Old Testament is in poetic form. Biographical and historical prose occurs, sometimes added by a later hand. But the basic message is usually in poetry. In addition to the normal aids of biblical scholarship you need some understanding and appreciation for poetry to grasp what is intended in such writing.

We do not know why the prophets wrote in poetic form. Since it is so, we can invent numerous theories as to why it should be so and some of them may even be right. But we do not really know why the prophet functioned as a poet. We do know quite well that there were court prophets and cult prophets, mantic seers, and witches in abundance in the ancient Near East. But so far as we know, they never wrote a body of poetic literature. With the other forms, such as story and law and wise sayings, we have considerable examples outside the Bible and even when the biblical types are quite different in purpose and form, the other literature is of considerable help in understanding our material. But with prophets as poets we start with nearly a blank page. In addition, scholars are not usually poets and so we have double jeopardy.

123

Having accepted these initial restrictions, we may now turn to some of the more common problems of reading any poetry. First, note how the prophet Hosea manages to convey an intense and conflicting set of feelings in a famous poem:

> When Israel was a child I loved him,
> > out of Egypt I called my son.
> The more I called them,
> > the farther they went from me,
> Sacrificing to the Baals
> > and burning incense to idols.
> Yet it was I who taught Ephraim to walk,
> > who took them in my arms;
> I drew them with human cords,
> > with bands of love;
> I fostered them like one
> > who raises an infant to his cheeks;
> Yet, though I stooped to feed my child,
> > they did not know that I was their healer.
> > > Hosea 11:1–4

Before all else, the poet has managed to convey an intensity of feeling about unrequited love by using these intense images. In the quotation from Hosea there is no doubt about the intensity of the feeling. The key idea, of course, is that God is a father. That is trite: the "father of the gods" is as old as literature. The unrequited love theme, however, is startling. That God should command is prosaic; that he should plead is disturbing, to say the least.

Then there is the feedback loop into the images. The images tend to be traditional as well as new. The father image is very traditional; the intimacy and tenderness are new. Then there are other traditional images, such as those of Egypt and Ephraim, which awaken a whole host of memories. Ephraim was traditionally the leader of the northern tier of tribes in Israel, a kind of elder brother. But then the contrasts emerge. To cast Ephraim in the role of a son who was being taught to walk is different. That God should stoop to feed his son is somewhat conventional; that they did not know he was their leader is paradoxical.

The phrase comes from an ancient tradition during the time in the desert when the people rebelled. The Father laid down a strict rule that they should never, never do that again. The finale of that instruction, however, is most odd: "For I, the LORD, am your healer." The parental experience of correction and reproof which is unpleasant and yet taken in stride, here breaks through any rigid application of theology.

The prophets seem at times to have been touched with poetic madness. Hosea's hearers said as much:

> They have come, the days of punishment!
>   they have come, the days of recompense;
> Let Israel know it!
>   "The prophet is a fool,
>   the man of the spirit is mad!"
>
> Hosea 9:7

The prophets have been called "the disturbers of Israel." They were not easy to live with; prophets in turn were often put to death, or at least rejected, in their own country. Jeremiah was not a run-of-the-mill citizen of Jerusalem; Amos was thrown out of Bethel as a threat to the government; Isaiah was told beforehand that nobody would listen to him; Ezekiel was the oddest of them all, surely mad to some extent. The visions were too large to be confined within one head.

Yet a word of caution must be said about the largeness of the poet's vision. Scientific language and our more normal logic attempts to put things in order. We proceed slowly from specifics to generalities or at least we test the generalities to be sure that we have left nothing out. Our final statement represents some sort of balance, perhaps even of compromise. The poet does not do this. The intensity of the feeling and the brilliance of the insights is concentrated; it is either totally one way or the other; at its best, it is both at the same time. But it is never a statement which can be reduced to a propositional form and cited as a general principle.

Amos said in a sudden burst of truthfulness, "If evil befalls a city,

has not the Lord caused it?" (Amos 3:6) There are other such statements
in the Bible which picture God as the God of death. Before we begin
to make a great conclusion from this, we should go back to examine
the intense feelings which were the birthplace of the insight. To those
questioning whether God could ever punish, Amos hurled his defiant
series of questions:

> Do two walk together
>   unless they have agreed?
> Does a lion roar in the forest
>   when it has no prey?
> Does a young lion cry out from its den
>   unless it has seized something?
> Is a bird brought to earth by a snare
>   when there is no lure for it?
> Does a snare spring up from the ground
>   without catching anything?
> If the trumpet sounds in a city,
>   will the people not be frightened?
> If evil befalls a city,
>   has not the LORD caused it?
> Indeed, the LORD GOD does nothing
>   without revealing his plan to his servants, the prophets.
> The lion roars—
>   who will not be afraid!
> The LORD GOD speaks—
>   who will not prophesy!
>
>   Amos 3:3–8

As a scientific statement or a theological argument, almost any
of these sayings can be contested. Surely people sometimes walk together when they are angry with one another; surely lions roar at some
other time than when they have seized prey; surely snares sometimes
malfunction; surely the prophets do not know everything God does;
surely there are evils in a city which the Lord has not caused. But this
is irrelevant. The intensity of the poet's feeling leads straight to a
disturbing but far-reaching conclusion: interpreting ordinary events as
ordinary is a capital crime. No prophet can keep quiet in the face of
such absurdity.

THE BOOK OF THREATS

The collection of poems called Isaiah is often divided into a Book of Threats and a Book of Consolation. The division does not work out very well in all particulars and yet the titles seem appropriate and so are generally used. The same is true for most of the other prophetic books. Instead of considering biblical poetry under such usual headings as lyric, epic, ode, elegy, and so on, I propose to make a simple division into poems of threats and poems of consolation. A somewhat similar method of analysis has been employed in the Psalms with good effect—hymns, thanksgiving Psalms, laments. What follows shall in large measure bypass the technical aspects of metre, rhyme, rhythm, and so forth, since they are largely lost in the translation.

The first chapter of Isaiah is used here as an example; it has the advantage of being one complete poem and in general estimation gives an epitome of the Isaian teaching. The text is not quoted here; you will need to read Isaiah 1:1–31 in the translation which you are using and refer back to the verses as I comment upon the poem.

The first decision you should make after you have read the poem is: What is the feeling of the poem as a whole? Let me suppose that some such phrase as "fury controlled by love" generalizes the feeling and then let us test this. Fury comes across quite clearly in the crescendoes which are employed. Verses 5 to 8 heap up images first of a sick man and then of a devastated city. Verses 11 to 14 reject sacrifices in general, then rams, fatlings, calves, lambs, goats, new moons, festivals, and so on. Verses 21 to 23 hurl against Jerusalem such epithets as adulteress, murderers, rebels, thieves, takers of bribes, those who fail to defend the widow and orphan. These crescendoes sound a note of doom; indeed, the last series (although it cannot be detected in the English translations) is one of the few identifiable Hebrew metres, that of a dirge. The passion is unrestrained; it is furious denunciation.

Yet the poem also conveys a feeling of great control. Irony plays a strong part and irony is a controlled passion. Verses 2 and 3 set the tone: "Sons have I raised and reared, but they have disowned me!" The expected is contrasted with the reality, culminating in that most sharpened barb: "But Israel does not know, my people has not understood."

In the tradition the Lord had never expected his people to be achievers, but he had expected them to learn. Knowing is one of those key words in the Bible which begins with the story of the Garden of Eden and runs through the Covenant relationship which was based on a very earthy knowing between God and people. The lack of knowing is further illuminated in the vast irony of verses 9 and 10 which are the end of one stanza and the beginning of the next. Except for a remnant, they have become no more knowledgeable than Sodom and Gomorrah in matters of religion. So they are called princes of Sodom, people of Gomorrah, traffickers in the sacrifice business. They have treated God as no better than the commercial gods of Sodom and Gomorrah, and this leads to that crescendo of rejection which we have already noted. Verses 24 to 26 state the great irony that the God of vengeance is vengeful against his own people and shall punish them in the hardest way of all by making them live under honest administrators. The whole poem ends with the irony that the strong man shall turn limp as a rope and his achievements shall only provide fuel for the fire. The sayings are extreme indeed, but the rhetorical form of irony clearly conveys the message that the poet has his material well in hand; he may be extreme, but he knows what he is doing.

Finally, the poetic form retains a hold on the love and concern of the Lord for his people even amidst the greatest excesses of feeling. In the midst of the condemnation a single exclamation, "Ah!," conveys the feeling that the Lord does not like what he is saying (cf. verses 4 and 24). The second crescendo is followed by a calm passage: "Come now, let us set things right, says the LORD" (cf. verse 18) and the irony of verses 24 to 26 is followed by a sad omen of redemption: "Zion shall be redeemed by judgment" (verse 27). This plaintive note dominates Isaiah. In some ways redemption is almost the worst thing that can happen and there is always a sober note to the statement.

This much can be noted simply by reading the English text attentively. You may also be impressed by the statements which begin: "Says the Lord . . ." (cf. verses 18, 24 and the modified form in verse 2). Scholars have traced the introductory and immediately following expressions through ancient diplomatic correspondence and legal procedures and term them either the "messenger formula" or the covenant lawsuit. This adds clarification to what we already suspect: the "Says the Lord . . ." statements are central. The ancient diplomat was given a specific threat to deliver and then allowed a certain leeway as to how it should be said, how it should be expanded, and how the negotiations should be moved along. So the "Says the Lord . . ." introduction and the immediately following statement are the gist of the prophet's message; the rest is the elaboration of the prophet himself. However, the difference between the biblical and the secular diplomacy should also be noted. There is no evidence that diplomats in ancient times spoke in poetry. The poetic format does bespeak a different function. It will be noted in the passages we are dealing with that no specifics are mentioned. Princes are accused of taking bribes but no specific prince is accused of taking a specific bribe. The people are accused of superficiality in worship, but no specific dates, offerings, or names are given. Threats are made: Zion is to be left like a hut in a vineyard, silver is to turn to dross, Zion shall become like a tree with falling leaves. This is not legal language but poetic; it is the attempt to heap up picturesque details for the sake of feeling rather than for the sake of historical or legal precision which is to the forefront. The language of poetry is far more important for the understanding than is the language of law.

If the poetry cannot be made into legal or historical precisions, neither can it be made to speak the scientific language of theology. That there are theological or religious implications in this passage is obvious, but that individual statements used for building up the intensity of feeling can be transported verbally into a system of beliefs is beyond what the language will bear. One cannot, for example, simplistically transpose the poem into a prediction that sinners shall burn in hell (verse 31) or into a theology that sin shall be whitened over while remaining sin (verse 18).

Such considerations become acute when the threats are pushed to their limits. Many of the prophetic books contain large sections of fierce denunciation of foreign nations. The prophecy of Nahum is a relentless and untrammeled paean of joy over the destruction of Nineveh. "A jealous and avenging God is the LORD, an avenger is the LORD, and angry." (Nahum 1:2) The feeling of satisfaction over the death of so many people continues unremittingly until the end: "There is no healing for your hurt, your wound is mortal. All who hear this news of you clap their hands over you; for who has not been overwhelmed, steadily, by your malice?" (Nahum 3:19) Isaiah, Jeremiah, Ezechiel, Amos, Hosea, and others are not much softer. Nor is the sentiment confined to the Old Testament. The Revelation of John is not a prophetic book in the same sense as the ones we are discussing here, but it does have poems of threat which parallel the old prophetic material.

> Fallen, fallen is Babylon the great!
>   She has become a dwelling place for demons.
> She is a cage for every unclean spirit,
>   a cage for every filthy and disgusting bird;
> For she has made all the nations drink
>   the poisoned wine of her lewdness.
> The kings of the earth committed fornication with her,
>   and the world's merchants grew rich from her wealth
>   and wantoness.
>
> Revelation 18:2–3

There is worse in what follows. As with the Old Testament prophets the first consideration should be the identification of the intense feeling. The feeling is one of exultation over the defeat of the final enemy. So the next chapter begins with a victory song.

> Alleluia!
> Salvation, glory and might belong to our God,
>   for his judgments are true and just!
> He has condemned the great harlot
>   Who corrupted the earth with her harlotry.
> He has avenged the blood of his servants
>   which was shed by her hand.
>
> Revelation 19:1–2

The seer's feeling leads to the insight that the victory of God is complete and against all odds. Indeed, that is what the doom songs are all about.

It will be noticed that the Book of Revelation speaks about Babylon. That, of course, is a stand-in name since Babylon was of no immediate concern to the author. But so too was Nineveh in Nahum's doom song, and Tyre and Sidon and Sodom and Gomorrah and Edom and Philistia and Aroer, and so on, in the other prophecies. The names are also symbols. They are the concrete images which the poet uses to define the intensity of feeling. The historical detail is secondary except as it helps paint the picture. The evil is cosmic, everywhere, and nowhere worse than among those whom God calls his sons. But the triumph is equally inevitable and so much the more triumphant.

THE BOOK OF CONSOLATION

As the first chapter of Isaiah was used to illustrate the poem of threat, so the first chapter of the Book of Consolation (or Deutero-Isaiah as it is called) is used here to trace the pattern of a poem of consolation. You need now to read chapter 40 in Isaiah, verses 1 to 11; I suggest that you do so slowly, jotting down the images which impress you, trying to see how they are intertwined and defining what feeling you get from the chapter as a whole.

The feeling intended by the poem is stated in the first word: "Comfort!" Comfort comes from security. Security arises from knowing that the worst is over and that a benign power still controls all. So the introductory strophe (verses 1–2) uses images which traditionally were consoling. The hearers are still "my people"; the word is addressed "tenderly" to a people who now knows. The service of the Babylonian Captivity is over, at least by anticipation; the guilt has been expiated. The images convey the feeling of security.

This is reinforced in the second strophe (verses 3–5) by a dramatic image of a new Exodus which this time shall be easy and shall accomplish the revelation of the Lord to all mankind. The third strophe (verses 6–8), however, sets this against a realistic background of doubt; all of this has been heard before. By using a dramatic device of question and answer, the poet voices the fear that even if the word of God stands forever, mankind doesn't: "All mankind is grass." This in turn is answered by the concluding strophe (verses 9–11) that the message is certain. Verse 10 has the resounding ring of a proclamation which cannot be hindered: "Here comes with power the LORD GOD, who rules by his strong arm." Then the ancient image of the Great King (a proper title) as a shepherd is used to strengthen the care and personal concern of this vast power of God.

The message is in the feeling and the feeling is made up of lights and shadows. The ancient hopes are exaggerated to make them appear without any base alloy; they are expressed in the most exuberant and earthy terms. It is Jerusalem which is addressed, a Jerusalem which is a herald of good news. The cities of Judah hear the message of the returning King; the ancient image of God carrying his little son in his arms awakens new hope. Yet there is still the darkness, the doubts that the word of the Lord will be effective. This is common to the poems of consolation. A song of doom may be phrased in totally dark and somber shades without any letup; a song of consolation must arise out of desolation.

The technique is extremely frequent and needs to be noted as you read. The great poems of the first Isaiah called the Book of Emmanuel (Isaiah 7 to 11) are an intricate weaving of a triple prophecy, that of doom for Judah, that of doom for Assyria, and that of a boy-king to be called "God-with-us." The second part of Isaiah (chapters 40 to 55) is noteworthy for the inserted Servant of Yahweh songs. The overall context is a triumphal hymn to a cosmic God who judges and controls all of human history; the counterpointed Servant Songs portray a servant who must suffer and offer himself to death in order to expiate sins. The great prophecy of Jeremiah about the New Covenant (Jeremiah 31:31–34) is set in a context of total destruction of Judah. Habakkuk has a concluding canticle in which he pictures himself as cringing in fear while he listens to the hobnailed boots of the conqueror approaching, only to discover that even if all is lost he can still believe in God, "my saving God." (cf. Habakkuk 3) That part of the message is used by Paul in his Epistle to the Romans; indeed, it is the admitted keynote: "The just man, because of his faith, shall live." (cf. Habakkuk 2:4 and Romans 1:17) Then Paul goes on to describe the fearsome effects of the Wrath of God in human society.

As with the poems of threat, so with those of consolation; the

message is to be found first of all in the feeling, not in the specifics
of the images which are used to convey the feeling. The sample poem
from Isaiah 40 mentions Jerusalem and the cities of Judah; their restoration in actual fact is subsidiary to the thought of comfort in old
and remembered things more than in any historical restoration. In
terms of historical realism the restoration was never really a restoration
but something quite different; a Jewish outpost permitted by Persian
authorities. Endless images of caravans bringing gold and precious
gems to Jerusalem, kings bowing down before the King of Jerusalem,
prosperity without work, joy without sickness, endless marriage feasts,
and so on, are heaped up to convey the feeling. Even the moral qualities
are exaggerated and sometimes questionable. Jerusalem "has received
from the hand of the Lord double for all her sins." (Isaiah 40:2) That
hardly seems fair. There will be exultant cries over the defeated enemies
and joy to see them cringing. This, too, is part of the technique for
conveying intense feeling. So in the Book of Revelation there is a
similar poem of extreme feeling in the Hymn to the Lamb.

> Now have salvation and power come,
>> the reign of our God and the authority of his Anointed One.
> For the accuser of our brothers is cast out,
>> who night and day accused them before our God.
> They defeated him by the blood of the Lamb
>> and by the word of their testimony;
>> love for life did not deter them from death.
> So rejoice, you heavens,
>> and you that dwell therein!
> But woe to you, earth and sea,
>> for the devil has come down upon you!
> His fury knows no limits,
>> for he knows his time is short.
>
> Revelation 12:10–12

SUMMARY

What is said here of reading the prophets is certainly not all that
you need to know in order to do it understandingly. The usual infor-

mation which we have seen in the chapter on stories also needs to be applied. Although great poetry may be timeless, it helps to know something of the time and circumstances of the original writing. "Something" may be as much as we can know since the dating of prophecy is often very vague. Amos 1:1 dates his writing to the times of King Uzziah of Judah and King Jeroboam of Israel. That, however, comprises a forty year span between 786 and 742 B.C. when conditions were changing rapidly, especially toward the end. Then there is the other intriguing time indicator which might explain much more: "two years before the earthquake"; but we know nothing of this. So we have problems trying to reconstruct the exact religious and social conditions in which the prophecy was written. Nonetheless, the effort is worth the investigation.

Moreover, many of the original poems have been edited and added to. It is extremely difficult to get any precision in determining precisely what was added later, who did it, and when. The style, the sometimes defective condition of the text in Hebrew, the use of odd and archaic words (poets are inclined to do this), the formalized styles of diplomatic and court language, all these require the service of specialists in linguistics, source criticism, and form criticism. The results even then are less than definitive.

Taking all of this into account, there is still the question of poetry. You can do a good deal of this simply by reading with a discerning eye. What has been proposed here is relatively simple. The aim of poetry is to convey a strong feeling. That is the first thing to determine in reading it: Which feeling is the poet striving to convey? Poetic language establishes moods by means of images. What images are used? Which of them are rich with tradition? Which of them are new and creative? How does the poet want us to respond to these images?

When this has been done, we need to set the underlying insight into the context of the view of God and his Chosen Ones which has been developing through the ages and which now faces a new crisis. What is new? What is old? Here also we have need either of a good memory or the help of the biblical theologian who attempts to deal with the various themes in the Bible. However, your own appreciation of the prophetic message is also growing in richness as you read more, and you yourself shall pick up echoes of previous messages on your own.

Prophecy, like poetry, is deliberately unbalanced. It concentrates its intensity of feeling on one point. Hence it must always be seen within the total function of prophecy. A prediction of woe cannot stand by itself; a picture of untrammeled glory and joy is but one side of the vision. Both must go together or we have no true prophetic message. Sometimes the poem we read has both together; more often than not, we must look outside the immediate text to discern the counterbalancing other extreme. The ancient rule that no verse can be interpreted by itself is never in greater need of application than in reading the prophets.

EIGHT

Prayers

THE PLACE OF PRAYERS IN THE BIBLE

This chapter is different. There is little profit in telling how to read prayers in the Bible. If prayer is not said or prayed, it is not prayer. The actual experience is part of the understanding; the nature of prayer is such that it must produce a subjective response or it has failed as prayer. Like poems, prayers are creations of our feelings. In both cases feeling is more than surface emotion; it expresses our convictions, our beliefs, our insights into life set to action in some definite circumstance. Charles Borromeo prayed: "God save Charles or Charles will destroy himself." The purpose of this chapter is to attempt to help you understand how some of this has worked upon the biblical authors and how it may affect your own appreciation of biblical prayers.

Prayer forms a substantial part of the Bible. The Book of Psalms is the obvious example. These one hundred and fifty prayers were used largely as public cult in the Temple of Jerusalem. The Christian church took over this body of poetic prayer and shaped a good part of its new liturgy around it. The Psalms are the most frequently cited part of the Old Testament in the New and the prayers of the New Testament are often based upon it. The narrative sections of the Bible are frequently interspersed with psalms, canticles, reflective petitions, thanksgiving, and petitions as interpretations of the story line. The story of Esther in its original Hebrew version was a bloodcurdling account of Jewish reprisal on would-be persecutors. God was not mentioned at all. The Greek translator felt such a need to interpret the events that several prayers were written into the translated text. One reads:

> O LORD GOD, almighty King, all things are in your power, and there is no one to oppose you in your will to save Israel. You made heaven and earth and every wonderful thing under the heavens. You are LORD of all, and there is no one who can resist you.
>
> Esther C:2

The New Testament continues the practise. When the prophet Samuel was born unexpectedly to his aging parents, his mother Hannah broke into a song of thanksgiving:

> My heart exults in the LORD,
>   my horn is exalted in my GOD.
>   1 Samuel 2:1

The pattern is repeated by Luke at the birth of Jesus when his mother Mary is also portrayed as interpreting his unexpected birth in the same way:

> My being proclaims the greatness of the LORD,
>   my spirit finds joy in GOD my savior.
>   Luke 1:46

The whole Infancy Narrative of Luke is organized around three canticles of praise that explain the point Luke wanted to make in telling the events in the way in which he did. The Gospel of John opens with a hymn to the Word of God which anticipates the point of the whole Gospel.

The late wisdom writing of the Old Testament such as Sirach and the Wisdom of Solomon is given to extremely beautiful prayer-like meditations and Paul follows in the same tradition. The Epistle called "Paul to the Ephesians" is, in fact, cast in the form of a prayer rather than an instruction. In fact, all of his Epistles begin with a somewhat elaborate blessing called a *barakah* in the traditional Jewish term and usually end with a doxology or invocation of the three persons of God in the Christian sense.

The second function of prayer in the Bible seems to be to portray the lifestyle of the Chosen People in its response to God. We have already noted that the Psalms frequently addressed Yahweh as the Great King. There were Psalms for the celebration of his enthronement in the Temple and Royal Psalms commemorating the political enthronement of the reigning king. The king was God's ruler, his "son." But who was the king? Such Psalms seem to have begun with the monarchy in David's time, increased in magnificence as the monarchy declined, and continued to be sung for centuries when there was no earthly Jewish king at all. To whom were the people singing? It would seem that they were singing about themselves. A very early tradition recognized that each person among the Chosen People was responsible for true worship and faithful living according to the Way. The thought, dimly seen at first, re-emerged in Christian times. The most important Christian prayer began: "Our Father." It accepted the Father-son (or daughter) relationship. It admitted the total dominance of God's kingdom and accepted the personal responsibility for living in dependence on him and forgiving as he forgave. New Testament prayer centers largely on the dual admission of the goodness of God and the dignity of the human person. The prayer-epistle to the Ephesians begins:

> Praised be the God and Father of our Lord Jesus Christ, who has bestowed on us in Christ every spiritual blessing in the heavens! God chose us in him before the world began, to be holy and blameless in his sight, to be full of love; he likewise predestined us through Christ Jesus to be his adopted sons—such was his will and pleasure—that all might praise the glorious favor he has bestowed on us in his beloved.
>
> Ephesians 1:3–6

Prayer defined who the people were. It is this formative factor of prayer within the community which must be attended to in praying biblical prayer. There are but few personal prayers in the Bible. Prayer is either an interpretative understanding of how God has affected us within experience or it is an acknowledgment of need for him within the Chosen People. Oddly, the Chosen People does not become disdainful of others because of its strong self-identification. It is the consciousness of the difference which makes the outreach possible. Prayers for the nations or for the "other sheep" are as comfortable to the biblical writers as are prayers for the Chosen. "I do not pray for them alone. I pray also for those who will believe in me through their word, that all may be one as you, Father, are in me, and I in you; I pray that they may be [one] in us, that the world may believe that you sent me." (John 17:20–21)

THE STANCE OF PRAYER

It is a curious fact that most of the great religions have discovered that physical position has something to do with prayer. It may be turning toward Mecca or assuming the lotus position or getting on one's knees or raising one's hands, but there seems to be great symbolic need for such acts. Apparently what they symbolize is the inner, spiritual stance which we take toward God. If prayer is an attempt to establish a conscious contact with God, then the proper position of God and man in this effort seems to be an essential ingredient in determining whether anything is going to happen. It is not just any god to whom the Bible addresses prayers nor is it just any human being who prays them.

The God who is addressed in the biblical prayers is *our* God, the God of Israel, the God of the Fathers, or in the New Testament the God and Father of our Lord Jesus Christ. That kind of God is not everybody's god. The tradition which makes him *our* God is the burden of the narrative in the Old Testament and the starting point for the *our* Father in the New Testament. The starting point of prayer is already far in the past. Others may study the prayers or adapt them to their own needs, but the very way of addressing God in the Bible has already acknowledged a connection between him and us. So he is a special God who is known as special by the wondrous deeds he has already performed for his people. Whether Abraham or Moses or the prophets or Jesus

Christ are the ones who pronounce the prayers, the stance has already been determined.

Nor is the human response simply "one on one." For example, the Psalms were almost entirely prayers for or within the community. In other books of the Bible the prayers were accepted along with the other material since they reflected the community's belief. They defined who the people were. Prayer had a special place in this self-identifying process. So Paul says "No one can say: 'Jesus is Lord,' except in the Holy Spirit." (1 Corinthians 12:3) This is no esoteric statement about an odd psychological phenomenon of people talking in tongues; it is simply a Christian interpretation of the old truth that even prayer is impossible unless the Lord takes the first step in calling us. It is an action of the people of God who are a people of God simply because God has called them to that mysterious mission. Consequently, biblical prayer must be seen in the context of this particular people who respond to God who has chosen them as his worshippers.

This does, indeed, set up a strange situation for prayer; namely, that the God of all creatures must be contacted as the God of his people. It does in some way also make the odd demand that the one who prays accept the status of being segregated from others. "I shall be your God and you shall be my people" is an odd view of a religion which from first to last is for the benefit of all the nations. In some way which we also experience in other affairs, it is the difference which makes unity possible. The God whom the Bible addresses in prayer is a very odd God who could not be found by reason. There is a frequent implication in biblical prayer that God is not listening or that he seems powerless or that stronger forces are ruling the universe. This does not conform to an abstract system of theology, but it does respond to the moods of experience of prayer with which we live. The abstractions are helpful; they may even be right. But it is not the approach of those recorded in the Bible who sincerely prayed to him. They found him to be a jealous God, a passionate God, and that he would respond only to a passionate attempt to touch him.

Perhaps biblical prayer is different from our feeble efforts at prayer in another way—it is always aware of the cosmic stance of God and of us. Prayer in the Bible is not usually a petty matter of asking Daddy for some goodies. Prayer is a declaration of embattled worshippers that they will persist in being different. Their God was veiled in mystery, awesome in his works, unpredictable in his plans, not to be manipulated nor ignored, Father, Warrior, Lover, but always the Mystery. In our perceptions he does not seem to rule with mighty and immediately effective sway. "Our Father in heaven, hallowed be your name, your kingdom come . . ." is the Christian prayer above all else. Yet the kingdom has not come in any overwhelming way. "Give us today our daily bread . . .," and after so many centuries one third of the world is still starving. We have not been able to bring it off nor, apparently, has he. "But deliver us from the evil one . . .," from that evil which Paul called another mystery, "the mystery of iniquity," "the principalities and powers, the rulers of this world of darkness, the evil spirits in regions above." The consciousness of that mysterious Evil determines the biblical authors' stance toward God, full of confidence and yet also full of humility before powers so much greater than self. It is harsh, but it is real; it is intimate and yet it is cosmic. Perhaps Sirach is typical of the stance:

> Come to our aid, O GOD of the universe,
>   and put all the nations in dread of you!
> Raise your hand against the heathen,
>   that they may realize your power.
> As you have used us to show them your holiness,
>   so now use them to show us your glory.
> Thus they will know, as we know,
>   that there is no GOD but you.
>   Sirach 36:1–4

It is not a "nice" prayer, but it is typical of biblical prayer. In praying biblical prayers one must expect the shocking and the mysterious.

Appendix

AIDS TO BIBLE STUDY

Bibles for many age groups and special purposes are published. Some of these use the standard texts referred to in Chapter One; some of them are special translations for children, Sunday School classes, or special interest groups.

Bible aids come in a great variety from simple illustrated texts with study guides or questions to elaborate methods of serious study. The range is so great that you may do best either to browse in a religious book store or to ask a teacher of Religious Education. Your own church may publish excellent materials. Noted below are simply a few sources of a more general kind which represent different major religious groups or which have been used successfully for Bible discussion groups.

A Listing of Teacher/Leader Resources, Task Force on Teacher/Leader Resources, National Council of Churches of Christ in the U.S.A., 475 Riverside Drive, Room 710, New York, New York 10027.

Proclamation Commentaries (Philadelphia: Fortress Press). A series of six commentaries on the Old Testament and six on the New Testament geared to emphasize the liturgical readings and to stimulate discussion,

New Testament Message (Wilmington, Delaware: Michael Glazier). Individual book length commentaries on the books of the New Testament by Roman Catholic scholars.

Collegeville Bible Commentary: Old Testament Series and *New Testament Series*, (St. John's Abbey, Collegeville, MN 56321: Liturgical Press). These newly reedited pamphlets on one book or several small books are excellently designed for discussion groups since they include the biblical text, good introductions and commentaries and discussion aids.

Concordia Publishing House, 3558 South Jefferson Avenue, St. Louis, Missouri 63118 publishes commentaries on individual books of the Bible under the general headings of Adult Studies on Books of the Old Testament and of the New Testament. Concordia is a Lutheran publishing house.

Neighborhood Bible Studies (Tyndale House Publishers, Wheaton, IL 60187). This is a series of pamphlets on individual books of the Bible (not all are yet included). Each pamphlet has introductory instructions on how to conduct a Bible Study Group using this format. The pamphlets contain only meagre commentary but provide appropriate discussion questions for sections of the text.

UMBERTO M.D. CASSUTO, *Understanding Genesis* (Jerusalem: Magness Press, Hebrew University, 1965)

J.H. HERTZ, C.H., *The Pentateuch and the Haftorahs* (London: Soncino Press, 1972). This is sometimes used in Jewish Bible Study Groups.

HOW TO ORGANIZE A BIBLE STUDY GROUP

Bible Study Groups come in all shapes and numbers. If you are interested in getting a group started, here are some suggestions which have been tested by experience:

1.   Contact the people you think will be interested. This may be done through church auspices or simply as a private enterprise.

A group of between six and twelve seems to work best. With less than six the dynamic of differing viewpoints usually doesn't emerge; with more than twelve some people will get lost and not participate.

2. Set a definite time and date for the meetings. A series of six weekly meetings is suggested for the initial effort. Assure those who are interested that the meetings will begin and end on time. An hour and a half is a good length for the meetings. People who hire baby-sitters or have appointments like to know that they will be free to leave at a definite time.

3. Let it be known that this is a study group, not a social gathering. If the meetings are held in a private home, keep the amenities to something simple such as coffee and cookies.

4. Select a text of some sort and, if possible, use one Bible. The Aids to Bible Study given above indicate sources for good texts. The first chapter of this book has an evaluation of various translations of the Bible which will aid you in choosing what seems most appropriate to your group.

5. At the first meeting, get the group to agree on the format which you will use. If everybody has the text at the first meeting, simply assign a certain number of pages from the text to be read before the next meeting. Since the group is meeting to discuss and not to be lectured to, allow as much time as possible for the participants to express what they have gotten out of the text, what problems they have encountered, and what further insights they have had in the light of their own experience.

6. Someone should be designated as the group leader. The function of the leader is to arrange for the meetings, to get an agreement on the matter to be covered at the next meeting, and to stimulate the discussion. The initial meeting may be somewhat awkward until people learn that they can express themselves freely without fear of being put down. The group leader may need to stimulate the discussion by asking questions about the text or proposing problems suggested by the text. Specific problems are always easier to discuss than generalities. It may also be necessary for the group leader to keep one of the participants from taking over the discussion by diplomatic ploys such as promising to discuss the matter privately after the session is over.

7. In subsequent meetings the group leader usually needs to ask for nothing more than comments or questions about the matter which has been read. The group leader need not be an expert on the matter being discussed, but the leader should read more extensively

than the others in the group and be able to supply some input as required. It should be taken as a matter of course that problems need not be solved but simply recognized as problems.

8. An extremely simple method, if the above is not agreeable or effective, is to read the text in the group and stop wherever a difficulty appears.

9. This book has been used as the text for discussion groups. If this is done, I would suggest that the group leader begin the first meeting (after the house-keeping chores have been attended to) by having the participants read the Preface and discuss what they have gotten out of it. Next the group leader can give a run-down on what is in Chapter One. The assignment for the next meeting will be Chapter Two. To cover the book in six sessions, it is suggested that Chapters Four and Seven be combined.

Bibliography

SCHOLARLY MATERIALS

This bibliography is intended as a brief sampler for those who are interested in the more scholarly aspects of the Bible as literature. I apologize for not listing more of the works which I have found helpful (and for omitting good books which I simply do not know about). The following are listed with brief annotations to get you started.

KENNETH R.R. GROS LOUIS, *Literary Interpretations of Biblical Narratives* (Nashville: Abingdon, 1974). This is a collection of three essays on biblical literary interpretation and fifteen examples of application to biblical passages. Nine different authors share their insights, most of them from the viewpoint of literature.

JOHN MAIER and VINCENT TOLLERS, *The Bible in Its Literary Milieu* (Grand Rapids: Michigan: Wm. B. Eerdmans, 1979). Twenty-five biblical scholars discuss various aspects of the literary milieu of the Bible from technicalities of Textual Criticism and Literary Forms to the more general insights into the Bible as literature. Some of the best-known scholars, old and recent, are represented.

ROBERT ALTER, *The Art of Biblical Narrative*, (New York: Basic Books, 1981) and *The Art of Biblical Poetry*, (New York: Basic Books, 1985). These two excellent books seem to establish Alter as the foremost practitioner of rhetorical criticism in the Old Testament today.

LUIS ALONZO-SCHÖKEL, *The Inspired Word* (New York: Herder, 1965). Ostensibly a work on biblical inspiration by a Catholic scholar, this book includes very penetrating insights into the communication values of language and literature.

S.H. BUTCHER, *Aristotle's Theory of Poetry and Fine Art* (New York: Dover, 1951). Aristotle's essay on Poetry is a rather disconnected piece on drama, but its analysis of tragedy is still the place to begin for that subject.

EDWIN M. GOOD, *Irony in the Old Testament* (Philadelphia: Westminster, 1965). Good is one of the few biblical scholars to consider irony in terms of tragedy and comedy. Good is much dependent on Aristotle and the Western tradition.

ROBERT W. FUNK, *Language, Hermeneutic and Word of God* (New York: Harper and Row, 1966). In this excellent treatise Funk considers language as event and the influence of language on theology in parables and epistles.

MADELEINE BOUCHER, *The Mysterious Parable* (Catholic Biblical Quarterly Monograph Series, Washington, D.C.: Catholic Biblical Association, 1976). An analysis of parables in Mark which centers on the mysteriousness of the parables as a challenge to the reader.

ROBERT M. POLZIN, *Biblical Structuralism, Method and Subjectivity in the Ancient Texts* (Philadelphia: Fortress, 1977). One of the more readable books on Structuralism.

JAMES BARR, "Story and History in Biblical Theology," Journal of Religion, 56 (1976), 1–17. James Barr, a distinguished biblical critic, broke new ground for the study of biblical theology in this article which advocated that story rather than history should be considered the primary carrier of theological insights of the Old Testament.

Interpretation, 34 (April, 1980). This issue of the Journal of Bible and Theology contains four excellent articles on the Bible as literature.

Index

of Jerusalem Bible (JB), 8–9
King James Version, 10–11
of New American Bible (NAB),
8
of New English Bible (NEB),
7
of New Jewish Version (NJV),
11
Trito-Isaiah, 18

2 Kings, publication date of, 17
2 Samuel, publication date of, 17

U

Upanishads, 4

W

Wisdom, publication date of, 18

Of further interest

A Handbook of
Christian
Mysticism

AN INTRODUCTION TO THE CHRISTIAN
MYSTICAL TRADITION

by Michael Cox

The Christian mystical tradition is one of the richest in the world, yet for many in the West it has been obscured by other, particularly eastern, spiritual disciplines.

This widely-praised survey examines the nature of Christian mysticism and describes its development from the New Testament to the flowering of Carmelite spirituality in sixteenth-century Spain. It also considers Protestant mysticism, the mystical element in English literature, and mysticism in the modern world as exemplified by two contrasting figures — Teilhard de Chardin and Thomas Merton.